Toffee Apple

Must Do Better In Love

Paris Connolly

Toffee Apple
Must Do Better In Love
ISBN: 978-2-492620-27-0
Text, Photo (Nice Beach), and Illustration
by Paris Connolly

Paris Connolly is Australian. This book has British spelling.

369FAD7410574CCC458009758186ACEF05FBFFDBFEDD5DE82F0E2A482BEEF174

"A man cannot be comfortable without his own approval."

— Mark Twain

CONTENTS

Chapter 1

'I asked my boss if I could have some extra hours,' said Cameron, hanging his arm around my shoulder.

My mother's Central American eyes flew to the arm. I stopped breathing.

Cameron kept talking. 'He reckons he might,' he said, with his arm hanging around my shoulder.

My mother's eyes got blacker by the second. Nobody in my family touched each other. There were no kisses, no hugging, no tugs of hair, no strokes of cheeks, no tongues in ears, no nothing. Zero, zilcho, nada. Except for smacking, that was very much allowed. Yet, here we were, this blue-skied Brisbane day, with birds in the back yard flying from the banana tree to the guava tree, standing in my kitchen smelling of over-ripe paw paws which were sitting in the ugly brown ceramic bowl I'd made in highschool, with my Australian boyfriend touching me with his bloody big arm.

The boy kept talking. 'He said he's going to throw any extra work my way. Good, hey?'

The arm. It was still hanging around my shoulders. Jesus Christ, the weight alone was enough to kill me. I was carrying the shame of a touched woman. I could hear my mother's thoughts, *"Just like a prostitute, she stood there and let him touch her. Has she slept with this boy? Is she a woman now?"*

My heart beat very fast. I had felt this type of terror before, playing cards with my father. When we were kids, the weekends had been Dad's turn to have my brother and me at his house. The house was set on a large block of land with two trees at the front. The bigger tree was my brother's and the smaller one with the Hawaiian-like flowers, was mine. Down the road from the house, there was a little beach where we'd go to poke bug-eyed, puffy fish with sticks.

The evenings at Dad's place were the adventure because if you needed to pee, you had to put your shoes on, grab the torch, and go outside. The toilet was on the other side of the back yard in a wooden shed, and you needed the torch to dodge toads. Once in the toilet, you had to scan for crawling, slithering, or hopping things too. The night adventures didn't last forever though because my father installed an inside bathroom a few years later and the word 'sawdust' was never said again.

The house was like my father, simple and rather English. On the weekends, Dad served us cucumber slices with cups of tea, and we played cards at his fold-up table. One day, I was so engrossed with my cards that when Dad played his killer card, he took me so much by surprise that I shouted, "Oh, you PIG!" before I could stop myself. At once, I took in a sharp breath, lowered my eyes, and sat frozen. It took three full seconds before Dad burst out in a great bellow of a laugh. The laugh was so loud and so sudden, that the Rosella parrots outside flew from their leafy tree branches, which were my leafy tree branches.

To be fair, perhaps the card terror was not quite the same as the Cameron arm terror. This day in the kitchen, I was struggling to breathe and my Central American mother was a second away from combusting. Cameron, oblivious to the total shit-stir he was creating, was smiling from ear to ear. Together, my mother and I guided chitty-chatty

Cameron to the front door and as I said goodbye, I almost vomited a sigh of relief. Closing the door, I turned to my mother. The blood had drained from her face and she had turned whiter than my English father, most hard to do considering the man was transparent.

'I'll get back to the bathroom,' I said, tucking a long strand of hair behind my ear.

My mother slumped against the wall. 'Use bleach,' she said. 'I need to call Lydia.'

Three minutes later, I heard her speaking to her sister.

'Suficiente para matarlo,' I heard from the bathroom.

There it was. My mother on the phone, asking for a black magic spell to kill Cameron. That was twelve years ago.

Forward to present day, and halfway around the world, to London, the Kings Road in Chelsea. I strolled along wearing jeans, boots, and my Ralph Lauren coat. Everyone else was wearing Ralph Lauren too, or if not, Ted Baker, Dolce and Gabbana, Chanel, Alexander McQueen, or some up-and-coming designer. Why not? We were in Chelsea, everyone was beautiful and there were so many things to do; lattes to be drunk, antiques to be bought, and the farmers market to be invested in. I was on my way to Peter Jones Department Store to spray on each of their perfumes. I needed to start narrowing down my choice for when payday came. As I strolled past Boots Pharmacy, a man stepped out and bumped into me.

'Excuse me,' he said, holding his hands up in apology.

'Excuse me,' I said, my eyes lowered to the pavement.

The women on the Kings Road turned to look because the man was stunning. He was tall and elegantly dressed in a Versace suit. He had long slender fingers, moisturized skin, a chiselled jaw and a good set of hair, surely cut and blow-dried each week. All the women noticed Mr Attractive, except for me, I kept walking towards Mr Jones.

This had become my standard behaviour when it came to men. Any time I found myself in a guy/girl situation, I entered a self-created safe zone. Years earlier, in a bar in North Sydney, I was sharing a drink with a colleague who I seriously fancied. Actually, he was my boss. He was well-travelled, well-spoken, and well-well-well-handsome. More than handsome, he was clean-looking. He had clean skin, blue eyes, and short brown hair. I enjoyed looking at the neatness of the man.

Rather remarkably, I said to him, 'Who's your type of ideal woman?'

'You,' he said.

I looked from his piercing blue eyes down into my drink. I peered into that drink, closer and closer, suddenly fascinated with the ice. I moved that ice about with my straw. I dug a bit and the digging turned to excavation. Finally, I lifted my head and exclaimed, 'Did you see? They put cucumber in my cocktail!'

Unfortunately, this was not an isolated incident and my behaviour was not exclusive to Australia.

'Tom really likes you,' my friends said, when we lined up at the bar of a trendy East London pub, for yet more pints.

'How can you tell?' I asked, looking back to the chunky wooden table where Tom was.

'Are you serious?' Marilyn and her boyfriend stared at me.

'Yeah, how can you tell?'

'Because, Idiot, when he talks to you, he runs his hands through your hair,' said Marilyn.

'No, he doesn't!' I said.

Blind. I had taught myself to be blind.

Back to the lovely Kings Road in Chelsea. I am 35 years old, single, and when I say single, I mean I have never had another relationship since that nerve-wracking Cameron experience twelve years earlier. The years of living with my Latina mother's beliefs about men, sex and bodies, had seeped and lodged into my psyche. I was like an apple, a healthy whole apple. Yet with the years of alarmed black eyes, pleas to the Virgin Mary, and statements like, "Don't let them touch you," this apple was now covered in toffee. I had become the toffee apple, protected with my rock-hard layer. I had become man-proofed. Almost man-proofed. Not altogether man-proofed.

I had had one-night-stands, all alcohol-induced, and all followed by periods of guilt and disgust. I had the same conversation with myself time and again.

"I can't be trusted with alcohol. I have no morals, no standards. I could have been killed or raped. Stop drinking. I drink, I talk. Then I end up in bed with a stranger. And why do I never wax my legs in time? How is it that I can even have so much hair? What is my alcohol problem? Please stop drinking. It is not funny."

It was funny to my London friends. They loved hearing the details.

'And he drove you home on his bike? As in bicycle?'

'Yes.'

'At 3 o'clock in the morning? Over Putney Bridge? The two of you, drunk, doubling on his bike?'

'Yes.'

'What's his name?'

'Not sure.'

'What does he do?'

'Uhm.... computers.'

'Are you going to see him again?'

'I can't even look at myself. No!'

True to my word, I would never see my one-night-man again. Clearly, they were a twelve-hour maximum deal for me, and only to be enjoyed with copious amounts of alcohol. I suspect the alcohol ploy is used by millions, not just a brainwashed toffee apple. Sober people are brave people.

So, I remained the single girl at 35 years old. But for how long, was the question. Surely it was not possible to be scared of men, sex, and my body forever? Would I ever have a relationship, a real one? Like where you brush your teeth side by side, kiss each other goodnight, sleep in the same bed, talk and be friends, share friends, and when you go to parties, you lightly touch each other and say things like, "We, are going to the countryside. We, want to see the forest. We, had a great time, thank you. You, must come over to ours." Would I ever have this?

Enter Dot. Dot was a guest at the Chelsea hostel I worked at. She walked in wearing stripy-coloured jeans, short brown hair, and a crazy lazy smile. She was young, about 25 years old. I pegged her for a lesbian immediately. Judgmental? Me? What?

'Hello.' She smiled, holding a backpack over her shoulder. She had what I call, "a Matt Damon smile."

'Welcome,' I said.

'My name's Dot. I've got a reservation.'

'Yes. I've been waiting for you.'

I liked being Manager of this small hostel. Technically speaking, I was also the Chambermaid, the Laundry Lady, the Gardener and the Cook.

The hostel catered primarily for travellers, offering dormitory rooms, but it had a couple of "good rooms" on the upper floors, for "real guests". They came from all over the world, always intrigued by the architecture and delighted at how English the place was.

'It's quaint, isn't it?' they said in thick North American accents, looking at the narrow corridors.

'Yes.'

'It's very... charming,' they said, looking at the dated floral curtains hanging from the bay windows.

'Yes.'

'The room is so small! It's so... English. I love it!'

'Yes.'

The hostel attracted a relaxed clientele and, on the odd occasion, a celebrity. One particular English celebrity, let's call him Fred, stayed in one of the real rooms whenever he came for a quick London visit. He was a discreet man, but the same could not be said for his friends. I got woken up at four o'clock in the morning one time, by the repeated pressing of the front doorbell.

Throwing on my Primark dressing gown, I stormed down the quaint narrow English corridor to confront whoever was being so rude at this time of the morning. I flung the front door open to see three very tall men on the doorstep.

'Hi!' said the one on the right. 'Is Fred in?'

The men stood side by side and my weary eyes travelled from one to the other, from Alice to Barbie to Candy. They wore bright-coloured wigs, outrageous make-up and they were dressed in glitter tank tops, glitter skirts, and glitter high-heeled shoes.

The middle man, a beautiful black transvestite, started serenading the upper floor. 'Oh, Fred Darling! We know you're there! Come out!'

His sisters jumped up and down on the spot, clapping their hands and giggling.

I pulled my Primark dressing gown tight around me and took a deep breath. Glancing down the street to see if any of our good neighbours' lights were on, I whispered fiercely, 'Fred is not here and it's four o'clock in the morning!'

Alice, the one with the pink wig, said in what was a surprisingly deep voice, 'Please tell him we're here. We're here!'

'Yes!' Barbie and Candy jumped with glee, actual glee.

'No!' I said. 'It's four in the morning. Go away. Goodnight!'

I closed the front door and marched back to my room. Damn Fred and his transvestite friends. I had to be up in three hours to cook breakfast.

In the morning, I walked the narrow corridor from the kitchen to the breakfast room and slid a plate of beans, eggs, bacon, and toast in front of Dot.

'Bon appétit,' I said.

'Thanks.' She flashed me the Matt Damon smile.

My eyes had gone to Dot often during her week-long stay. I had snuck peeks at her in the mornings when she was getting ready to go flat and job-hunting, and in the evenings when she chilled out in the lounge with the others. I couldn't pinpoint what it was that was attracting me. She was of average weight and height, with pale skin and brown eyes. It was perhaps a combination of the Damon smile and her naturalness. She never wore make-up. Also, like many Australians in general, she was relaxed in nature.

'The job interview? Yeah, not bad,' she said, when I asked. 'The money's okay, the people seem okay. The woman said she'd let me know tomorrow. It'll be pretty cool if it comes off.'

Ms Cool-As-A-Cucumber had me discreetly studying her from behind my Full English Breakfasts. As I shot her smiles each day, I convinced myself that she was smiling back, as in "smiling back", and my thoughts revved into overdrive. Was the reason I hadn't been in a relationship because I had been looking in the wrong direction? Salmon swim upstream to mate. All my life I had been swimming downstream. Don't tell me I was a salmon?

"What's it like to kiss a woman?" my brain asked.

It predicted the answer, "It would be sexy, and ... hot."

I worked, I thought. I worked, I thought some more. Before long, I had convinced myself as to why I had never had a boyfriend since muscular-armed Cameron.

'I just might be a lesbian,' I said to myself in the mirror.

By Saturday afternoon, there was no other option.

I said to Dot, 'Let's get some of the others and have some drinks. It's your last night here. Let's celebrate your new job and your new place.'

'Okay,' she said, looking me straight in the eyes.

I felt secure to go ahead with my "kiss a girl" plan. How hard could it be? I strolled down the street to my local off-licence and got busy pulling bottles off shelves.

'Are you going to be able to carry all those bottles?' asked the off-licence guy, handing me my change.

I shot him a smile, and pointed to my trusty nana-trolley that I'd bought at the Fulham Road Markets.

On Saturday night, in my room, just about ready to join the party, I stared at my collection. 'I think,' my eyes scanned the pretty bottles, 'this is a N°5 night.' I picked up the bottle sitting between the Estee Lauder and the Cartier, and sprayed my neck and wrists. Holding my wrist to my nose, I inhaled and let out a happy Chanel sigh.

'Mica?'

My eyes went to the door. It was Cristal.

'Are you coming?' she said.

Looking at myself in the mirror, I gave a silent thumbs-up. My hair was blow-dried straight and tied in a ponytail. I wore my standard jeans, t-shirt, mascara, and lipstick. I held my wrist to my nose, inhaled, and walked out the room.

The breakfast room, aka the party room, was full of hostel guests aged between 20 and 35 years old. They were made up of three types, holiday-makers, workers, and just-back-from-traveling-must-find-work types.

Being the manager of this establishment with its revolving door of clients, I'd heard the same conversation between guests again and again. All of them were a version of:

'G'day, my name's Mark.'

'Nice to meet you. Brad.'

'You from South Africa?'

'Yeah. You from Australia?'

'Yep. What are you doing over here?'

'I'm on a working and surfing trip, hey.'

'Yeah? How does that work?'

'I work for six months, surf for six months.'

'Awesome. What work do you do?'

'I'm a supply teacher. It's okay, it pays well. What about you?'

'I'm a nurse, just back from travelling and now I have to work for four months. Got a massive trip to India planned, before going home.'

'Cool, Man. Where have you just been?'

'Spain, it's a cool place, hey. Went with a group of friends, one of us got arrested, one of us got robbed and the rest of us did okay.'

'Awesome. Whereabouts in Australia are you from?'

'A place called Wollongong. It's near Sydney.'

'I know Wollongong, I dated a girl from there. Justine Barker.'

'Justine? Tall girl? Primary School Teacher?'

'No way!'

'Yeah, I reckon! Small world, Mate.'

Small world indeed. The hostel acted as a United Nations social service. It provided the perfect environment for the creation and nurturing of embryonic friendships that would later grow into big fat healthy facebook friendships, maintained dutifully once each traveller was back in their respective country.

All the Marks and Brads of the hostel were more than adequately acquainted with the art of getting pissed on the cheap. The breakfast table was strewn with three-for-ten-pound bottles of wine, bottles of cider, beer cans, and Tesco crisps and dips, plus foil ashtrays, already brimming.

'Here's to your new home!' We lifted our plastic cups to Dot.

'Bayswater, eh?' said Stew, the guy who had been living at the hostel the longest. 'Not bad.' Stew pushed a strand of his greasy shoulder-length hair away from his face.

Dot smiled. 'Yeah, it's going to be cool.'

'When are you moving out, Stew?' asked Sally, joining in the conversation.

'No time soon, Mate,' said the gangly Antipodean. 'I like my Full English Breakfast.'

'Well,' Sally's face softened as she leaned in, 'Stew, there's this thing called a supermarket, and in it,' her New Zealand accent got thicker as she spoke, 'they have iggs, bacon, and brid. I'm not joking, you can buy this stuff and make an Inglish Brikfast yourself, in your own flat with your very own bedroom for you, hey!'

Sally's sarcasm confused long-term lodger Stew. He smiled crookedly. That's all he did.

I drank yet another cup of wine, while looking over at Dot. She was sitting at the end of the table in her stripy-coloured jeans. With cigarette in mouth and plastic cup in hand, I walked over to squeeze in next to her, but Nathan slipped in first.

'So, do you have cable in your new place?' Nathan asked Dot, his face close to hers.

Nathan was a surfer dude, just back from Biarritz. His blond tatty hair fell around his tanned face. As I stood leaning over him, my cigarette ash dropped down into his hair. He didn't notice. I looked around, nobody else did either.

'Pretty awesome living across from Hyde Park,' Nathan said to Dot.

A little more ash dropped into his hair. I looked at the cigarette in my hand and then down to the blond tatty hair.

"Don't do it," said my brain.

I looked at the cigarette.

"Don't do it," repeated my brain.

'Having a housewarming? I'm up for that.' Nathan invited himself over to Dot's new place.

'Fire!' I shouted.

The room stopped, all eyes on me.

'Where?' Stew came running, his thin arms gangling like a rag doll.

I pointed to Nathan's head.

Stew looked at the blond tatty hair, his eyes searching. 'What?' His blue eyes looked to back to me.

'What?' I repeated, waving my cigarette around. 'Where's the fire?' Stew shook my arm.

I pointed to Nathan's head again. Nathan looked up and put his hand on his head, confused. Frowning, he stood up and went to the bathroom. Stew gangled off, shaking his head, and I slid down into the seat, next to Dot.

'Hi ya.'

My friend, and also long-term lodger, Cristal came and sat opposite. A giant bag of Doritos lay on the table between us, like a sacrificial gift to the alcohol gods. We munched and drank the night away, never letting our cups get empty.

True to form, the drunker I got, the more I talked.

'Nana Mouskouri and Julio Iglesias, now there's a dynamic duo.'

Dot and Cristal endured bullshit story after bullshit story. I was not alone, everyone was drunk and rambling in southern hemisphere accents. We drank the place dry and filled the room with laughter and cigarette smoke.

About midnight, people started going to their respective dorms.

'I'm out. Ta for the evening. Good Luck, Dotty.'

'Goodnight.'

'Catch ya's at brekky.'

'Me too, night.'

'See you in the morning.'

'Night.'

I shifted in my seat more and more as each person left. This salmon was about to do a u-turn and it wasn't as easy it one might think. Each time I lifted my cup to my mouth, I took a discreet sniff of Chanel in an attempt to self-soothe.

'You okay there, Mica?' Cristal asked, watching me refill, again.

'Yep.'

'Have a Dorito.' Cristal pushed the near-empty packet over.

I pushed them back and drank my wine. Dot's hand was resting on the table. She didn't wear any rings on her fingers and her unvarnished nails were cut short. Leather bracelets looped her wrist. I lifted my hand and placed it over her hand, and without skipping a beat, or even looking at me, Dot curled her fingers around mine.

Miss Cristal didn't miss it. She stood up. 'Well,' she said, her eyes glancing at our love hands, 'Goodnight.'

Through red wine eyes and a haze of cigarette smoke, I watched Cristal leave the room. She was the last person to go. I looked at Dot. Dot looked at me.

'Mica? Mica?' Cristal banged on my door the next morning. I turned my throbbing head. Dot lay fully clothed on my bed, sleeping. My brain searched for memories. The kiss! How was it? Total blank. I couldn't remember it. Total, complete and utter blank. How inconvenient. I had to imagine what happened. I had horrific visions of me with red wine lips and red wine teeth grinning at her, and lunging for her like an undersexed, plump teenager. Shit.

'Mica?' Cristal banged the door.

I looked at my clock and jumped. 'Coming!' I washed my face, brushed my teeth, flung my hair into a pony, changed t-shirt, one squirt of Beautiful, and shoes on. I looked back to the sleeping girl on my bed. I wondered how far we had gone. Not that far, we still had clothes on. What was it like? Was it hot? Or were we geeks? Fuck my relationship with alcohol, fuck it! And fuck my hangover. I flung open my door, looked at Cristal's bemused face, and flew down the narrow English stairs.

'Good morning!' I breezed past hungry guests in the breakfast room, including tatty-haired Nathan.

In the kitchen, I turned on the stove, laid out the bacon on the grill, cracked a few eggs in a bowl, and drank a can of ice-cold Fanta in two goes. Burping out alcohol breath, I put my hand to my head. No kiss memory. No memory past the point of holding hands. I searched the drawers for painkillers, found them, and swallowed them.

After the guests finished breakfast and the room was empty, I opened the windows, waving stale smoke out to the streets of pretty Chelsea, and I drank as much Fanta as

I could. As I was putting away the worn-out floral place-mats, I looked up to see Dot, showered and dressed in jeans and a singlet top. Her face was free of make-up and it was expressionless. There was no smile, but no grimace or frown either. Her overstuffed backpack was on the floor next to her.

'Hey,' she said.

'Coffee?'

'Thanks.' She smiled weakly and sat at the same table where the deed had happened. Assuming it had happened, that is. We didn't say much. We couldn't, the hangover.

She pushed her mobile phone across the table. 'Put your number in.'

I punched my number in and pushed the phone back.

Taking her phone, she stood up and said, 'See you.' She hoisted up her backpack and walked out of the hostel.

My head was trying to catch up with my eyes and register that my girl kiss had just disappeared when the phone rang. I got a fright and jumped. I ran to the kitchen and picked up the phone.

'Duke's Hostel, good morning.' I faked a smile to sound less hungover.

'Mica?' my sister's voice came down the line, 'it's me. Can you talk?'

Mango had figured out the best time to call me from Brisbane was post-breakfast time, my time. This should not be undervalued, her mathematic skills are not her strong point.

'Yes.'

'Guess what? Remember Susannah? Well, her younger sister Veronica is a you-know-what.'

'What's a you-know-what?'

'A girl who... you know.'

'No, I do not.' I put my hand up to my throbbing head, praying for the paracetamol to kick in.

'A girl who likes girls. You know.'

'Oh! I believe you are trying to say that she is a lesbian.' My eyes flew towards the door Dot had just walked out of.

'Yeah!'

There were certain words my older sister couldn't bring herself to say. These included Lesbians (you-know-whats), Drugs (thingies), and Vagina (your thing). Just a little hiccup she has. I understood. Our childhood upbringing did not include labelling things correctly. It did include labelling men as dirty and dangerous however, and those girls who you know, you had to watch out for them too. Can't have the man, can't have the woman. It would appear I was in a spot of trouble. Luckily for me, I lived on the other side of the world and my twisted, nut job, Central American family would never find out and put spells on me or burn me on a stake. Right?

Chapter 2

'She wants a date!' I said, studying the text. I made the same excited face as when I was a kid and I heard the Mr Whippy van.

Cristal stubbed her cigarette out on the cement courtyard step. 'Go on a date, kiss her, and remember it. No alcohol.'

My head shot up. 'No alcohol?'

I wore Paloma Picasso perfume for our first date, which was at midday at an 'All You Can Eat' Chinese Buffet Restaurant in Shepherd's Bush shopping mall. There was a Pound Shop on the ground floor. I peeked inside as we walked past. A woman stood, counting the money in her purse to see if she could add the toothpaste she was holding into her basket. The basket was already full and a packet of chocolate biscuits, similar to Digestives but not Digestives, lay on the top. From the look on the woman's face, it was a choice between a sweet tooth or a clean tooth. I never knew the result as we stepped onto the escalator and rode up to our half-empty restaurant.

The Chinese buffet was a good choice. Food is probably what we had most in common.

'Shall we go again?' said Dot, lifting her empty plate.

'I'm right behind you,' I said, sucking up a stray noodle.

It was easy to relate to her. We shared the same cultural references.

'My father got the belt, and he chased my little brother around and around the back yard, for like, fifteen minutes,' she told me.

I laughed, shoving a piece of honey chicken into my mouth. 'And?'

'My little brother was too fast. He kept running around in circles. Eventually, Pa gave up.' She imitated her father, "Don't think you're off the hook! You're gonna do all the yard chores for a bloody month!"'

'And, did he?' My eyes crinkled with laughter, listening to her descriptions of Australian country family life.

'Too right. What Pa says, goes.'

I felt pangs for Australia and days of running around huge back yards, chasing friends, trying to wet them with the hose.

Over lunch, Dot continued her Australian stories, and I sat up paying attention, loving the way she mimicked family and friends in her strong country accent. I laughed easily and often, and by the time she had told her third Pa story and I had gotten round to the Braised Beef and Noodles, we had bonded very well.

At the end of the date, we stood outside busy Shepherd's Bush tube station.

A preacher stood on the corner, shouting to the stream of people exiting the tube.

'May the Lord shine down on you, my brothers and sisters. You are loved. Let's love each other.' The man raised his hands up to the sky, speaking more to his Lord than to those around him.

I wasn't ready to love this girl standing next to me, but I was really rather curious and willing to start with a kiss. I looked over at her. She was standing with her hands in her jean pockets. She stood smiling at me. Suddenly, something was wrong. I squirmed. She seemed too sweet, too nice, and too girl. I shuffled back.

"What the fuck are you doing?" my brain said, my eyes looking at her soft girl face.

I looked around me trying to buy time, whilst holding my wrist to my nose for some Paloma Picasso.

The Jesus Preacher still held his arms up to the sky.

When I turned back, Dot was still looking at me, but this time giving me "the look".

"Ah," my brain got it, "10-4. Copy that. I'm receiving you. Over and out."

That evening Cristal and I spread out our Waitrose microwaved meals in the breakfast room.

'Well?' said Cristal, smelling her curry chicken.

'No kiss. Just a peck on the cheek.'

'Did you ask if you two kissed the other night?'

'No!'

'So you don't know?'

'I don't know.'

'You're rubbish.'

'I know.'

'Maybe you're just friends? Are you sure she likes you?'

'She gave me the look.' I stirred my £1.99 Shepherd Pie ready-meal.

'Do you like her?'

'She's funny.'

'Are you attracted to her?' Cristal re-phrased her question.

'I'm intrigued. I want to have a bit of fun, just try, see if I'm a salmon.'

'Go again. This time use alcohol,' Cristal said, mixing her rice with the sauce, 'but pace yourself.'

Dot had moved into a flat in Bayswater with friends, and our second date was at a traditional English pub opposite Hyde Park.

'Two pints of cider, please,' I ordered at the bar.

There was no pacing. The pints flowed non-stop, and so did Dot's funny Australian stories. My head fell back as I laughed harder and harder. Her eyes lit up as she appreciated my attention, but there was no touching or special looks. It was just two friends enjoying many pints on a Friday night in London town, much like half of the city's population. It was only when we finished the evening with a drunken criss-crossed walk along the park that Dot reached and took my hand. This was London, no-one could care two hoots for girls holding hands, but for me, inside, my drunken nerves danced. It was time for the second kiss, provided that there had been a first one of course.

I'm embarrassed to say I cannot remember the second kiss either. My mind simply was not going to register this. It was like it was on my mother's orders, "Don't let her remember one single second of this crazy behaviour. No no no no no no!"

This was not good. I couldn't remember the first or the second time we kissed. I remember my first boy kiss to this day. I was a seventeen-year-old exchange student, spending a year in southern Spain. The village, full of white houses with red-tiled roofs, was set amongst fields of olive trees. I really liked eighteen-year-old Javier because he sang and played the guitar. Javier really liked me too, but he had a girlfriend. So I kissed eighteen-year-old Andres instead, in a nightclub that had a dirt floor and an orange tree. The next day when I saw Andres he had hickeys all down his neck; big fat red love bites given by me. I must have been a vampire in a previous life. I blushed when I saw him. I still blush now, thinking how I must have been crawling over him and sucking and sucking and sucking at his neck. The poor guy looked like he'd suffered some extreme allergic reaction. At least, later in the year, I did get to kiss Javier, and it was lovely. No hickeys involved.

Although I don't remember the second girl kiss, I remember my feelings. They were of surprise, that her face was soft and her lips were soft, and her hands too.

'Soft?' said Cristal, opening her microwaved chicken and chorizo soup.

'Yeah,' I said, peeling the plastic off my Waitrose salmon mornay ready meal.

Cristal's face squished up.

I nodded. 'Yeah, I know,' I said, 'but she's really cool and so easy to be with.'

Cristal's eyebrow lifted. 'Uh huh,' she said, her tone flat.

'And her friends are really fun.'

'Uh huh.'

'And Bayswater is fun, lots of cool restaurants.'

'Uh huh.'

I continued my defence. 'It's only playing, short-term. Everyone knows I'm moving to France soon.'

Cristal picked out a piece of chorizo with determination. 'Does she know that?'

'Yes, I told her. She knows. She knows.'

For the first few weeks when I visited the Bayswater flat, I acted like there was nothing going on, in front of Dot's curious flatmates' eyes.

'Hey,' I'd greet Dot, in front of her flatmates.

She'd walk towards me, going for the kiss on the lips. I'd turn my head, and she'd kiss my cheek. The flatmates looked on, brows burrowing.

I could hear the unspoken question, "Why is she pretending? We know!"

Dot and I had of course kissed more by this stage, my memories intact. Kissing was fun, as I thought it would be. It was the thought of breasts which were proving to be a struggle. My thoughts swung around in my head, and they floated there like the floating smelly smoke the catholic priest swung around on a chain in church. I never understood the smelly smoke stuff and I definitely didn't understand the breast stuff.

My mind managed as best it could. "I don't think I can go there. No? That's okay. Just kiss. She's fun and nice. Don't worry about the breasts. Anyway, this is going to fizzle in a week or two. You're moving to France. Yes, I'm moving to France. Good. Good. Relax. Yes. Yes, I will. Good. Good."

Everything was relaxed, or so I thought, until one of the Bayswater Flat Brigade pulled me onto their small smoking balcony one day.

'What are you doing?' whispered Dot's flatmate, lighting a cigarette.

'What?' I lit my cigarette, sucking in menthol, looking at the balding pigeon near my feet. It was the skankiest pigeon I had ever seen; skinny, losing feathers, walking nervously. Looked like it had done years of crystal meth.

'With Dotty, what are you doing?'

I shrugged. 'I'm having fun.'

The stupid pigeon thought my ash was food, it kept coming closer.

'You're not gay.'

'I'm just having fun,' I whispered. I kicked the air, and the skank jumped back, but didn't fly off.

'She's falling in love with you.'

'No, she isn't,' I whispered, smelling my wrists. 'She knows this is temporary.'

Later in Dot's bedroom, she presented me with a red gift-wrapped box. 'Open it,' she said.

I looked at it.

'Open it,' she repeated.

'Nah.' I shook my head.

'Don't be silly,' she said. 'Open it.'

I peeled off the wrapping. 'A purse?'

'To replace yours which is falling apart,' she said, squeezing me tight.

Two nights later, my friend Marilyn and I stood at the bar in a tapas place just off of Oxford Street. We were celebrating Marilyn's birthday. She looked over at Dot, standing at the other end of the bar.

Marilyn said, 'Watch out. She's already jealous.'

I laughed, picking up a chunk of tortilla, at the same time noticing the well-dressed barman. 'No, she isn't!' I said.

'She's planning the wedding. Better get your family lesbian-prepared.'

I shook my head. 'My family will never be lesbian-prepared, plus no need to be, cause they are never going to find out. This is good tortilla.'

'Try the calamari.' Marilyn pushed a little plate over.

Sensing someone looking at me, I turned.

Dot stood at the end of bar. 'Hi,' she mouthed.

I nodded hello back, before turning back to Marilyn. 'Okay,' I said, 'I'll pay more attention.'

'I'm only telling you as a friend,' Marilyn said, picking up the calamari. 'Come on, let's join the others.'

'La Vida Es Un Carnaval' was playing, and I followed Marilyn, swinging my hips and glancing back to see if the barman was watching me.

For the rest of the evening, I was on Dot Alert.

'Did you see it? I went to see it last weekend, it's good,' I said to Malina.

'Yes, and I loved it,' said Malina, holding her sangria.

'I haven't seen it yet,' said a voice behind us.

Malina and I turned to see Dot standing there.

'There's Richard,' I said, pointing. 'I'll be back in a sec, just have to ask him a question.'

I left Malina and Dot to mingle.

'Thank you. Come over, have a look at it, and I will make us dinner.'

'But will you make us dinner?' said Richard, tilting his sarcastic head to one side. His brown eyes looked massive through his square, black-rimmed glasses.

'No, you're right, I won't make us dinner. I will buy us

dinner and serve it lovingly, as a thank you for fixing my computer.'

'When are you making us dinner?' said a voice from behind.

Richard and I turned around. Dot was holding her glass of wine, looking from me to Richard.

Marilyn came dancing past, placing a fresh glass of sangria in my hand, winking, and dancing on.

Stumbling home along Oxford Street later that night, Dot said, 'You know I'm here for you, Mica.'

I stopped in my tracks, outside Boots Pharmacy. I caught a glimpse of shiny stuff in the window. Estee Lauder was on promotion. I made a mental note. Looking back at Dot, I suddenly saw it, I saw the change. How had I not noticed? She had gone from being cool and relaxed, to being needy.

'You know I'm going to France in two weeks? You know that, right?' I looked her in the eyes.

She laughed nervously. 'Yeah.'

'Good.'

We continued our drunken walk and as we reached Bond Street tube station, I noticed her eyes brimmed with water. I frowned. Crying? Growing up in my family, if you cried, you got hit. Always.

'Waaah waaah waaah,' I cried to my mother, 'I hurt my knee.'

'I told you not to go out in the yard!' Thump! The big smack came.

There was never a different ending to the story.

'Waaah waaah waaah, I lost my dolly.'

'You should have been more careful!' Thump! The big smack came.

I was slow to learn.

'Waaah, waaah waaah.'

'Why are you crying?' my mother asked.

'Waaah, Kelly is moving to Sydney, it's not fair.'

'Kelly is moving and you're crying? I'll give you a reason to cry!' Thump! The big smack came. Before I could get away, she said, 'And another one!' Thump!

I did eventually learn.

So, I was bewildered when I saw tears from Dot this night. I looked closer, double-checking the tears were really falling. I bit my bottom lip. She kept crying, and we kept walking in silence. This was too much for my drunken self to be dealing with.

My heart surprisingly seemed to have an opinion on the matter. "I feel weak. Make her stop," it said.

My head had a different opinion. "No, ignore her."

I had a sudden urge to thump her. I clenched my fists and kept walking. All I had to do was make it through this night, and I promised myself, tomorrow we would be over.

I had slept over at her place before, and I'd surprised myself by finding it easy to sleep next to her, which didn't help me with my confusion.

In the middle of the night, I stirred, trying to open my dry mouth. In the darkness, I fumbled for the water on the bedside table.

'Baby?' Dot woke from her sleep. 'You okay?' she whispered.

'Yeah.' I gulped my water and snuggled back down.

Dot nestled in behind me. 'Mica, stay with me, at least till you go to France, okay?'

'Nel Blu Di Pinto Di Blu' pumped out of my MP3 player as I jogged down the road and waited at the lights. I had a one-hour midday break from my job, and I needed to run it out. 'Push The Button' came on as the green man came on. I ran over and across Albert Bridge to Battersea Park. I jogged along the river. My eyes swept from the boats and brown water, to the people rollerblading, playing tennis, kicking balls, and riding bikes. People's lives were flowing, but my life didn't seem to be flowing. 'It's A Kind Of Magic' came on. I turned left, over Chelsea bridge and left again along the embankment, dodging large brown leaves on the ground. Something had gone wrong in the relationship, but rather than just end it, I had decided to let it fizzle out to my leave date. I knew I'd made a bad decision. I had turned into one of those immature people, the type that string people along rather than just end the damn relationship. What a chicken-shit coward. I scratched the back of my neck. Jogging around the corner into my street, 'All Fired Up' came on. Pat Benatar, now there was a sexy woman.

'Promise me, no touching and no looks!' I gave orders to Dot that evening in the Chelsea kitchen, pointing my finger, exactly how the nuns at my highschool used to when giving warnings.

'I promise, just friends,' said Dot.

Cristal chopped the carrots and celery. 'So how do you know her?'

'She's friends with my sister. I know her and her husband, they have three kids, but I haven't seen them in years,' I said, taking the wine out of the fridge.

'And she's travelling over on her own?' asked Cristal.

'No, with a friend, I think.'

The doorbell rang. The girls looked at me. I waited for one of them to move.

'I'll get the door, shall I?' I said, rolling my eyes and pushing past them to run upstairs.

Tina stood with her arms outspread. 'Mica! Great to see you!' We hugged. 'This is Roger,' said Tina, her hand going to the man next to her.

Roger looked like he was in a rock band. He wore jeans and an old t-shirt, and he had shoulder-length black hair, and strong arms.

'Hello, nice to meet you,' I said. 'Come in, come in. Come downstairs and meet my friends.'

In the breakfast room, Dot and Cristal stood side by side. They had finished laying out the table with the carrot and celery sticks, the houmous, the olives, and a bottle of wine. I made the introductions, and we sat down.

'How is David? And the kids?' I smiled at Tina.

'Good thanks, Mica. My kids are getting big, you wouldn't believe it.'

My eyes took in the changes in Tina. When we knew each other, she was an adolescent. Her hair was curly and frizzy, her skin was patchy and her teeth were yellow. Now she was a very attractive woman with straight glossy hair, creamy skin, and a beautiful smile.

'You look great, Tina.'

'Thanks,' she said, patting down her hair.

'Your eye make-up is great,' I said.

'Thanks,' she said, blushing.

'Life is good for you,' I continued. 'What's your secret?'

The pink colour flushed her cheeks again. 'Oh you know, just finally taking time for me.'

'Keep doing it. It suits you.' I raised my glass.

With the pleasantries of, "How is your sister? How is your mother? Where are you living now?" out of the way, the conversation turned to Tina's visit.

'I didn't do it before I got married, so now is my time for my own trip. And Roger happened to be free the same dates as me, perfect travel buddy!'

'What about Madame Tussauds? Have you been yet?' I

asked, picking up a fat olive from the farmers market.

Tina put her hand on Roger's knee. 'We, have been meaning to go. But we, haven't managed to yet.'

All eyes went to the knee. Tina's face turned pink for the third time.

Roger sat up straight. 'Do you recommend it?' he asked, his voice trying hard to sound casual.

'I recommend it,' said Dot, also trying to sound casual.

'I've been too,' said Cristal, hurriedly. 'Go early to avoid the queues.'

'More wine?' I opened the second bottle.

As I went to fill Dot's glass, Dot put her hand over mine.

'I have an early start in the morning. I better head off.'

Tina's large eyes darted from Dot's lingering hand, to me. Fixing with a perfect smile, Tina said, 'How did you two become friends?'

At that moment, I could see the wooden stake being prepared by my family, and I could feel the heat of the flames that were about to scorch me to death. I scratched the back of my neck.

'Dot was a guest at the hostel,' I said, looking into curious Tina's beautifully made-up eyes.

'Oh,' said Tina, smiling.

Roger looked at his hands, saying nothing.

Dot said nothing.

Cristal looked from me to Tina, and from Tina to me, a smile glued to her face. 'I-I-I live here,' she said. 'Hey, Mica?'

Tina had her eyes on Dot. 'Where do you live, Dot?'

'Bayswater,' said Dot quietly, standing. Dot looked at me and said, 'I've got to get going. I've got to work early in the morning.'

I glared. 'Then you might want to say goodbye to everyone, not just me.'

It was Dot's turn to turn pink. 'Goodbye, lovely to meet you.' She said to Tina and Roger as she backed out of the room. She nodded to Cristal. 'Goodbye Cristal. Goodbye, er, ah, thanks for the evening.' Her voice trailed as she backed out the room.

Tina looked at me. 'She's nice,' she said, her fake red nails tapping her wine glass.

'Yes.' It was my turn to tap my fingernails. Flashing Roger a brilliant smile, I said, 'Roger, I'm guessing you know David, Tina's husband?'

Cristal stood. 'I will, just, er, go and refill, er, these uhm, carrot sticks.'

Tina and Roger didn't stay much longer and Cristal went to bed soon after they left. I packed the dishwasher, took the sausages out of the freezer to defrost for the morning, and went to have a shower.

'Merci, mon Dieu,' I whispered to the ceiling as I climbed

into bed. My move to France was just around the corner. I fell asleep with Jacque Brel's voice and song swirling in my head, 'Ne me quitte pas'. I was definitely going to quitte her, quitte her, quitte her, quitte her.

Chapter 3

Crusty, itchy psoriasis had erupted on the back of my neck, and the more I stressed, the worse it got. With days to go till I moved to France, my stress levels were mounting, and they were not helped by Dot's crazy-talk.

'My friend at work is gay. She says it has taken her girlfriend ten years to get her head around being gay,' she had said the night before.

My eyes had widened like a spooked horse's and I'd searched the dressing table for the Gucci, sprayed both wrists, and inhaled. 'I'm leaving in four days,' I said, one eye on her, one eye on my suitcase in the corner.

Tears had spilled out of her brown eyes, down her make-up free face, and over her puffy lips. I clenched my fists. Right on cue, my phone had vibrated. It was a text from my sister, Mango.

"They're taking Veronica to the priest."

Veronica's family had decided she needed the church to pray away the lesbian in her, it seemed. I wasn't surprised, and I know Mango wasn't. Mango knows what it feels like to be taken to the priest.

My sister is twelve years older than me and I remember my mother taking her to the priest when she turned eighteen, not because she thought she was a lesbian but because doubt had been cast on her virginity. My mother thought an Australian Catholic Priest was the right person for verification and to put things back in order, so to speak. A Catholic Priest! She dragged my crying sister all the way to the presbytery to shame and blame, and when they got there, she pushed Mango before a mild-looking white man in robes and spat out the words, 'Mi hija es una mujer hecha y derecha.' As if that wasn't humiliating enough, my sister had to translate for the white man. I don't know what happened next. We never talked about it. Seriously though, a Catholic priest, to purify my sister? A Cath-o-lic Priest?!

It was at this time that my mother ramped up the anti-penis brainwashing, to make sure she never had to take me to the presbytery. "Always wear tight jeans. It will be harder for them to take off, when they rape you," was her latest piece of wisdom. I'd nodded in young obedience.

Picking up my phone, I'd replied to Mango. "Lucky for V, the priest will be sympathetic as he very well may be in a similar position."

Four days later, the Big Goodbye was not such a big goodbye after all. It was more an Efficient Goodbye. Cristal and Dot stood at Victoria Station and with a quick kiss on the cheek for both, and a respectful nod goodbye toward my trusty Costa Coffee kiosk, I swung my heels around. With my back straight, eyes forward, I trolleyed my luggage through the gates and along the train platform, overtaking the slower passengers. I didn't look back, not even when I reached the doors. Inside the bleak train carriage, I put my luggage in the hold.

A voice came over the tannoy. 'This train will be stopping at East Croydon and Gatwick Airport. Doors closing.'

Three hours later, I took the final UK goodbye steps.

'Welcome on board,' said the flight attendant, taking a giant step back from me.

I had had forty-five minutes before boarding and had raided Boots Pharmacy for a last-minute perfume hit. Chanel, Versace, Estee Lauder, Gucci, Cartier, and Dior had all gone on my wrists, up my neck, down my chest, and behind my ears.

With my daypack patted into the overhead compartment, I settled into my window seat. The man beside me started sneezing. I looked out my window. My dream of living, as a single heterosexual woman, in France, was beginning.

"Oui! Moi, lesbienne? De quoi tu parles! Moi, hetero. He-ter- o."

I had studied six months of French in high school. Ironically, our French teacher was a lesbian. She was a glamorous, red-headed, French-speaking lesbian, or so the rumour went in our all-girl Catholic school. Ten years later, I went to France to work a ski season as a chambermaid and I fell in love with the country immediately. France is where I feel at home. I allow myself to sink into the crazy gorgeous spectacular beauty of the country. How is it possible for a country to be so visually pleasing? I find pleasure in the language too, I have ever since those grade eight lesbian classes. When in France, I'm a talking machine, I don't shut up. I talk to the postman.

'Bonjour Monsieur.'

'Bonjour Madame.'

'Il y a une lettre pour moi?'

'Pas aujourd'hui, Madame.'

'D'accord. A demain, Monsieur!'

I talk to the hairdresser, the local Chinese restaurant lady, and the tabac man. The words, the lovely French words, all of them, make me happy, even the word 'catastrophe'. I listen too. I listen to French radio, Cherie FM, a station playing yesterday music. I watch television too. My eyes shine as I recognise television personalities seen on previous trips to France.

Years earlier, I had worked a summer in a hotel in the hills behind Cannes. The hotel sat on a large piece of land, reasonably distanced from the many magnificent neighbouring villas. I was in awe of the villas, and curious about their owners. Who were these people driving shiny cars up winding driveways, having family Sunday lunches of fresh bread, foie gras, and Rose, on terraces by their swimming pools? These people have space to breathe, space to wake up and just breathe. These people wear expensive perfumes and white linen shirts. I wanted to be like them so badly! I wanted to come home after work, drive up the long gravel driveway to my open-space, artistically decorated villa and have a glass of chilled Rose by the goddamn pool, with some olives from my mate's olive fields, and some saucisson from the local butcher, who happened to be the godfather of my child who I dressed head-to-toe in white linen. I wanted to breathe in the wealth in the air of these South of France hills, and of these beautifully maintained gardens that you couldn't see from the road because they were fenced off by manicured bushes and an iron gate at the driveway entrance.

Our hotel had large iron gates at the front too, but no guard dog and no luxury garden. It had a swimming pool though, one we weren't allowed to swim in. We, the hotel staff, a mix of Brits, French, and Germans, had the beach instead.

'Have you put the jams away?' Jenny asked in her Manchester accent.

Standing in the breakfast room, which looked out to the swimming pool we weren't allowed to swim in, I slapped my head. 'No, I'll do it now.'

'Hurry up,' said Jenny. 'Meet me in reception in five minutes.'

'Okay, go go go.' I shoo-ed Jenny away and raced for the strawberry, raspberry, and apricot jams, covering them in film and putting them in the fridge.

I ran to my room, wriggled out of my uniform, threw on my bikini and a throw-over dress, and grabbed my beach bag. Jenny and I ran out of the hotel gates and up the hilly road. We had the routine mastered because if we missed the 11 o'clock bus, we had to wait one hour for the next bus to take us into Cannes.

'The big dog's coming up,' said Jenny, as we ran, getting closer to a beautiful Spanish-style villa.

'Yeah,' I said, running. 'Run fast. Ready?'

Holding our beach bags tighter to our bodies, we ran fast, past the gates. The black dog was waiting and barked non-stop. I caught a glimpse of his angry eyes and drooling mouth. Even though he was behind bars, I always thought he might jump through the manicured hedges on either side of the gates. He never did, and Jenny and I always arrived at the bus stop on time, but slightly traumatised.

Once in Cannes, we strolled through the streets, stopping to look at souvenir and clothes shops, before walking past the port and getting to "our beach" and "our spot".

'Now then, that's our spot. Put your towel down,' Jenny said in her northern accent. Looking to the water, she always said the same thing. 'It's dead nice, isn't it?'

Jenny wore a tiny bikini with a g-string bottom. My bikini bottom was less string, and more healthy-piece-of-material. We read our books under the sun, listened to the sounds of splashing water and light chitter-chatter, and every now and then, we went for lazy swims to cool down in the dead nice water that I could stare at forever because of its chalky blue colour. At four o'clock we gathered our stuff to catch the bus back, travelling through pretty hillside villages till we got to ours. Again, when we got to the Spanish-style villa, we ran fast past the dog, to the safety of our hotel, in time to shower and start dinner service. This was our daily practice, and as the sun kissed my skin each day, it wasn't long before I radiated absolute health and my soul beamed with utter contentment.

Each Saturday night, the hotel staff gathered in Jenny's bedroom because she had the big television. We took our low-cost rum that we'd bought in the village supermarket, and crisps that we'd stolen from the hotel. We squashed up on Jenny's huge bed and watched Star Academie, the French equivalent to Pop Idol. Drunk, brown, and happy we sang our hearts out, encouraging the contestants and boo-ing the judges.

'What did he say? What did he say?' we asked.

Sandrine, our French co-worker, translated. 'He say she sing like a pig.'

'He did not say that!'

'No. He say she need more time, no now is no good.'

Everyone nodded and heads turned back to the television for the next contestant. With cheap drinks and stolen snacks, this was a cultural experience of the low-cost sort, yet so rich.

Apart from the South of France hilly scenery, the blue-sky weather, the white linen, the smile from the woman in the post office who never normally smiles, the Star Academie music and television programmes, I adore what so many others do in France, the food.

'Bonjour Madame.'

'Bonjour Madame. Puis-je avoir une baguette et un pain au chocolat, s'il vous plait?'

'Ce sera tout?'

'Oui, merci. Non! Um... et un chausson aux pommes.'

'Tres bien. Ce sera tout?'

'Errrrrrrmmmmm...,' my greedy eyes scanned the counter, my teeth bit my bottom lip, 'oui, merci.' I had to remind myself that I could always come back for more. No need to buy everything at once. It was still going to be there tomorrow.

'Ladies and Gentlemen,' the voice came through the speakers in the plane, 'we will be landing in fifteen minutes, please fasten your seatbelts. The temperature in Nice is twenty-three degrees and the time is fifteen past eleven. We hope you have enjoyed your flight. Thank you for flying with us.'

I readied myself for landing and for my next South of France adventure. The smile never left my face as I looked out the window at the blue, blue, blue sea.

On day two in Nice, I left my hotel room carrying a piece of paper with the address of a studio for rent, not too far back from the beach. The studio was advertised as privately owned by an older guy. When we met, I was immediately wary because he talked too much of the charm.

'You're Australian? Oh, I've been to Australia. Beautiful, of course. I love Australians,' he said, leading me up the stairs.

My wariness went out the window when my eyes saw the balcony and the view.

The studio was on the top floor of a small apartment block. It was a large space with white walls and a white-tiled floor, and its view of the sea was spectacular, stretching from the airport across to Nice Centre. The expanse of sparkling blue water had an instant effect. Smack, bam, boom! I stood on that balcony, my eyes capturing, my pulse slowing and my heart melting.

The view of course, was the big plus of the studio. The minuses were that the kitchen hot water tap didn't work, and the toilet was a machine toilet. When you flushed, a loud motor started. It sounded like you were revving up to mow the lawn. Also, the balcony, which was the same size as the studio, was dangerous because it wasn't properly enclosed. It had half-finished, rusting railings. On top of this, the private owner got dodgier and dodgier as we spoke.

'If anyone knocks on your door, you say you're my cousin visiting me.'

I looked around. The tap, the toilet, the rusting balcony rails, and the landlord... every single thing about this flat was dodgy. All the warning signs were there.

'I'll take it,' I said, ripping the pen from his hand to sign a six-month lease.

The day I moved into the studio, I discovered my dodgy landlord lived on the floor below. Too late, I'd signed the lease, and I was far too happy with my Mediterranean view to be put off.

'If you want to make a little extra money, you can cook for me every day,' he said, trying to follow me into the studio.

I blocked him at the door. 'No, thank you.'

'Nothing fancy. Just steak and vegetables.'

'No, thank you,' I said, closing the door. I walked out to my balcony and stared at my view.

My Sud de France routine developed immediately, easy-peasey lemon squeezy. Lazy morning wake-up, stretch, check the sky was still blue and the sea was still twinkling, put the coffee on, clothes on, brush teeth and run downstairs to the bakery.

No matter what time I went, there was always a queue out of the bakery onto the street. The people waited quietly. I spent my time in the queue on tip-toes, stretching to look inside, tilting my head every now and then because I started doubting my predictable croissant order. This was because of the way they presented their pastries. It was as if they employed a visual artist to showcase the croissants, pain au chocolats, chaussons aux pommes, pains aux raisons, brioches, palmieres, croissants aux apricots, millefeuilles and gigantic meringues. Individually the little pastries were beautiful enough, but collectively, to die for. In fact, so beautifully displayed were the pastries that had the bakery been a women's clothes shop, I would not have walked in. I would have been intimidated, thinking the shop was too expensive and too luxurious for me. My local bakery was proper high class.

The beauty of the display was not the key component however, the key component was the smell. Smells of butter mixed with divinity, nurture, and 'I've got to have it', wafted out. Impossible to ignore. Who can walk past a bakery smelling of buttery divinity? Sure as hell not me.

I doubted my choice in the queue each morning, sure I would veer off the worn path and order a chausson aux pommes or a croissant aux apricots, but when it came to my turn, I remained loyal.

'Prochain!' A matronly-looking sales assistant called me forward. 'Madame?'

'Bonjour. Un croissant et une baguette, s'il vous plait.'

Back up on my dangerous balcony, I enjoyed my croissant with blueberry jam and a coffee. Then I typed my emails and played on the net. At lunchtime, I devoured the baguette with paté de campagne and salted tomatoes, and drank more coffee. In the afternoons, I skipped along the Promenade Des Anglais to the beach for a well-earned swim, and on my way home, I stopped via the mini-mart to grab a half roasted chicken and a bottle of red for dinner on the balcony. Each night, I looked around my new surroundings. Motor toilet or no motor toilet, I was definitely in heaven. There was an unexpected bonus too. My new lifestyle, together with the seawater, had cleared up the psoriasis behind my neck!

One late afternoon I relaxed on the chaise longue on my dangerous balcony, looking past the rusty half railings, hypnotising myself with the view. I picked up my phone and dialled. 'Cristal, I'm looking straight out to endless blue sea.'

'Yeah?' said Cristal. 'I'm looking out at the basement window bars. Up on the street, a dog has just taken a piss on our gate. And it's raining.'

'You're blessed,' I teased her. 'Come over when you can, you'll love it. I want you to come. I want all my friends to come.'

To my right, I looked out over at Nice airport, sitting on the sea. I could see planes lining up on the tarmac. When a pilot friend had come to visit me, we had sat on the balcony and with her back to the airport and she had listed what type of plane was taking off, just by the noise it made.

'That was a 747.'

Over the next month, thoughts of London floated away. Not all thoughts, I had changed my opinion on relationships. I shocked my friends and myself by proclaiming, 'I can't imagine not being in a relationship now.'

I remember Marilyn's reaction. 'YOU can't imagine not being in a relationship?'

I had to agree, even I was amazed. I had liked the safety of that short London relationship, the feeling of having someone look out for you.

Mango, thankfully unaware of my gay phase, had texted, "Maybe you'll meet a nice French fella in Nice?"

Maybe I would. Just maybe, maybe, maybe, I would finally have a real boyfriend.

Dot texted me from the UK frequently, of course.

"Hey Baby, how are you doing over there?"

My replies to her were bland. I remember a friend once saying she thought her boyfriend was going off her.

'How do you know?' I'd asked.

'Cause I'll text, "Hey Gorgeous, what are you up to?" and he'll text back, "Hey Mate, nothing much."'

'Mate?'

'Yep, Mate.'

My texts back to Dot were like that, lots of, "Nothing much, Mate."

On my solitary walks along the Promenade Des Anglais, I noticed couples everywhere. They could have been friends, but little things told you they were a couple. It could be a hand outstretched to protect her from the oncoming cyclist, a smile shot at him as he said something pleasing, a second look to check in with a beach decision, a laugh, an offer to carry the beach bag, a cheeky shove, a gentle placing of a cap on his head, a hand to wipe away the hair blowing in her face, or a passing of a water bottle. I sighed, brushing away my own strands of hair from my face, getting my own water bottle.

I was on my balcony early one evening when the phone rang.

'I'm coming over for a visit,' said Dot.

'Are you?' I asked, staring out to sea.

'Yes, I want to see this beautiful beach you talk about.'

'It's not all beautiful,' I said, looking at my half-finished rusty balcony railing.

'Which airport do I fly into?' she asked.

'Er, er, ah, ah...' I had a chance to block this.

'Is it Nice?'

'Er...'

'Mica, I just want to see this gorgeous place that makes you so happy.'

'Well...'

'Come on, just as friends.'

I sat up straight on my chaise longue. 'Really? Just as friends? You're okay with that?' My smile widened as I looked around my paradise, thinking how nice it would be to share it.

'Yes!' I heard her smiling on the other end.

My smile grew.

'I'll spend six weeks with you before I head back to Australia,' Dot said.

'Six weeks?'

That same evening I was on the phone to Cristal. Her tone, as usual, was flat. 'Even a blind person can see it, Mica.'

'She has to fly back to Australia after six weeks. I think her visa runs out. She's not allowed to overstay it,' I said, scratching the back of my neck. I added my favourite words, 'It's only temporary.'

'Even a blind person can see it,' repeated Cristal as she hung up.

Selfishly, I was looking forward to having Dot come and stay. I wanted to share my Sud de France experience.

My phoned beeped. New text from Mango.

"Maria-Louisa is travelling through Europe. Gave her your address. Going to stay with you. Tell me when she gets there. She's not spoilt anymore. Love you."

My hand started scratching the back of my neck.

Two weeks later, I stood in my studio, preparing myself for Dot's arrival the following day. My anti-tears armour was being put in place and my heart was steadying itself. I reminded myself again of the frustration I had caused myself by not being honest, and I promised, "No more of the lesbian games." I could not afford the mental energy it took to be in a relationship with her. It was too confusing and too exhausting. I had disappointed myself in London because I could see how selfish I had been. I had had two strong personalities occupying my mind.

The first personality had thought, "Where are your balls, your decency? You know you are wrong together, you feel you are wrong, yet you stay. She gives, you take. You, my dear, are a selfish shit. Could you be any more emotionally under-developed?"

The second personality had said things like, "Lighten up, for fuck's sake. Dot wants to be with you and it's only till you go to France. Stop being so dramatic. God, you're boring me."

Confused, I hadn't been able to see anything, except my own watery-eyed devotee who adored me. And I adored being adored.

The night before Dot's arrival, I paced up and down my studio chanting, 'I promise to not be a selfish shit. I promise to not be a selfish shit. I promise to not be a selfish shit.'

The next afternoon, I walked into the airport. Dot came through the gates, her face make-up free and her skin, white. She was in contrast to me with my tanned skin and wild curly black hair. She dragged her backpack towards me, with tears in her eyes. My smile froze when I saw the tears.

'I'm not going to cry,' she said, reading my thoughts.

'No, you're not,' I said, giving her a warm hug.

She forced a smile and held out a Duty-Free Bag. A little something Versace twinkled at me.

'Thank you,' I said. 'Come on. Let's go.' I led her out of the airport. 'Wait till you see the toilet!'

Back at the studio, she went straight to the balcony.

'Wow,' she said, her eyes digesting the view, 'it's brilliant!'

My eyes gleamed at her approval. I opened a bottle of red and laid out some paté de campagne mini toasts on the little plastic balcony table.

Dot said, 'I can see why you love it here. It is seriously beautiful.'

My heart doubled in size.

I passed her a glass of wine. 'Welcome to the South of France!'

'Thank you,' she said, taking a big swig. She took a mini toast. Her head nodded as she savoured the paté. 'Very good.'

My smile took over my whole face. 'Isn't it?' Pride oozed out of my pores, as if I had made the wine, the paté, and the view myself.

I stretched out on my chaise longue.

Dot's eyes looked at my bare legs. 'You've gone really brown.'

'Yep.' I looked over at her legs. 'We're going to have to get you some 50 plus cream.'

She laughed. 'Yeah.'

We drank red wine all afternoon. For the evening meal, I served my mini-mart chicken with a fresh lettuce and tomato salad.

'This looks tasty,' said Dot, picking up her fork.

The mini-mart was a six-minute walk from the studio. They had fresh fruit and vegetables displayed on the pavement, next to a rotisserie, with skewered chickens going around like a little ferris wheel for chickens. I had discovered the mini-mart on one of my first walks to the beach. With each subsequent walk to and from the beach, I took note of the times the chickens would be ready, because there was one disappointing day when I'd skipped down, purse in hand, only to find the chickens still turning.

'Encore trente minutes, Madame,' the mini-mart man had said.

'Trente minutes?' I hung my head and walked back home and my stomach had bitched the entire six-minute walk back.

'Yep,' I said, 'everything is tasty. Wait till you try the croissants.'

Dot's eyes looked from left to right. 'Where's the bakery?'

'Just downstairs,' I bragged.

'Oh Baby, yes!'

My back straightened. She didn't linger on the word, nor did she try to make eye contact.

'More wine?' she asked.

I opened a second bottle of red whilst looking up at the sky. It was slowly getting darker, reminding me that when nighttime came, we would be sharing my sofa-bed as friends. My hand went to the back of my neck. I looked over at Dot, vainly expecting her to be looking at me, but she was gazing at the view. I poured the wine and relaxed back into my chaise longue.

We lazed our way through the second bottle, catching up on gossip.

'Nathan got fired,' said Dot.

'Surfer Nathan from the hostel?'

'Yeah. He was supposed to turn up to work, but had tickets for the footy, so called in sick, but when he called in, his boss could hear the footy announcements in the background.'

'He called in sick, from the stadium?'

Dot nodded and laughed. I started laughing too.

'And remember Stew? Stew had to spend two nights in hospital,' said Dot. 'One of his patients was stealing the hospital spoons and Stew confronted him about it, and the guy flipped out and attacked him.'

'What?'

'Yeah, he punched him in the face and the groin.'

'What?' I tried to keep the smile off my face. 'Stealing spoons? In the groin?'

Dot laughed. 'It's funny now, but it was pretty serious. The groin is no laughing matter.'

I burst out laughing.

Sighing, I looked over at her happy face. It felt like we had reverted back to the two friends who met at the Shepherd's Bush All-You-Can-Eat Chinese restaurant. We were just two friends who loved food, wine, and talking. I hugged my empty wine glass. The night air was breezy, and my head was woozy.

'Bed.' I stood, looking out at the view. The twinkling sea had become black. All the fish must have been bumping into each other in the dark. There would be no bumping into each other for us. I was no longer a salmon.

Dot grabbed the bottles and glasses. 'Yeah, I'm knackered.'

She brushed past me, accidentally knocking me off balance. She quickly caught me by my waist and pulled me against her body.

'Sorry, are you alright?' Her familiar face was very close to mine.

I shrugged her off. 'Yep,' I said, walking inside.

Dot dumped the plates on the bench and went past me to the bathroom. I filled the sink with boiling water from the kettle and quietly chanted to myself, 'I promise not to be a selfish shit. I promise not to be a selfish shit.' I got six chants in, when I heard the lawnmower go off.

Moonlight filled my little studio. Dot jumped into the squeaky, uncomfortable, thin-mattressed sofa bed and looked at me. I was standing by the other side of the bed, biting my bottom lip and looking over at the two empty bottles of wine.

Dot patted the bed. 'Get in, Mica. Just friends, right?'

Chapter 4

Downstairs from the studio, there was a pizzeria on the street corner. It had a little window on the side street for people picking up takeaway orders and near the window, there was a doghouse and a bowl of water. I walked past the doghouse, turned left at the corner, past the front of the pizza place, and stood in the queue for the bakery.

Four minutes later, she called, 'Madame?'

'Bonjour Madame. Deux croissants et deux baguettes, s'il vous plait.'

I walked back past the doghouse to my top-floor studio holding my bread and warm croissants, knowing that I would also eat a chausson aux pommes later for afternoon tea. I knew this because greed was in my nature. It started as a child. I was the winner when my brother and I had the watermelon contest.

Our Brisbane back yard was a veritable fruit and vegetable farm. Banana, fig, paw paw, and guava trees thrived, grapes hung down from vines, and lettuces, tomatoes, chokos, and herbs pushed up in the vegetable patch. Along the back of the house, lemon trees, chilli trees, even more tomatoes, strawberries, and watermelons grew. We had loads and loads of watermelons.

'Let's see who can eat the most watermelon in one go,' suggested my teenage brother, Beebee.

I was younger, but greedier. 'You're on.'

The competition started in the kitchen. When Beebee yelled 'Go!' we had to race outside past the barbecue, to the shady side of the house, pick a watermelon, carry it back to the kitchen and eat it as quickly as possible, using a tablespoon.

This was no real competition because Beebee, after eating only two-thirds of his watermelon, wiped the juice from his mouth and pushed the melon away. He refused to eat another tablespoon. Not realising that as soon as he conceded defeat I automatically won, I kept on spooning watermelon into my greedy, piggy, gobble-guts mouth until there was no red left in my melon. I felt extremely sick for the rest of the day, but even that didn't cure my bad case of greed.

When my sister married and had two toddlers, we took them to the Big Pineapple on the Sunshine Coast. You can see the farm in its entirety if you walk inside the giant fibreglass pineapple at the entrance and climb the many stairs to the observation deck.

Mango's boys were very young and very well-behaved on the visit. I wasn't. My teenage stomach could think of nothing but The Big Pineapple restaurant and its tantalizing, massive ice-cream desserts topped with fresh cream and macadamia nuts. Before we got to the restaurant though we had to do a tour of the farm, riding on the little train which meanders through the fields, with pineapples to the left and pineapples to the right. The boys loved it, but I was impatient to get to the banana splits. Greedy girl grew up into a greedy adult and was now living in the South of France above a high-class bakery.

Back up on the balcony, with the croissants, coffee, blueberry jam, clear blue skies and twinkling sea in place, Dot and I gave respect.

'They're the best bakers,' I said. Flakes of precious croissant fluttered down onto my plate.

'Absolutely incredible.' Dot focussed on spreading her jam.

Breakfast was followed by the beach. Things were checklisted first.

'Mats? Shoes? Books? Water? Sunscreen? Yes? All good? Let's go.' I tucked my foam mat under my arm and we set off.

Downstairs, the pizza dog had arrived for the day, which meant the pizza guy had arrived for the day. The chocolate-brown dog lazed in front of his doghouse, his red tongue happily hanging out.

'Bonjour Dog,' I said.

'Bonjour Dog,' said Dot.

We turned left, past the pizzeria and the bakery, skipped across the road, and zigzagged through the palm tree-lined streets.

At the Promenade Des Anglais, we waited to cross the busy intersection. There were loads of Vespas on the road, many driven by teenagers. Parents must have been economising for the day.

'Papa, I'm 16, I need a car!'

'Do you know how difficult it is to find parking in Nice? Where are you going to park a car? No.'

'I need to get around. I need to get to my boyfriend's

house.' She pouts as she checks her mobile phone. No new messages. Papa looks at the adolescent. Adolescent continues, 'And er, er, to go to school, to tennis, to English class, to Grandma's house, to...'

'Ça va, ça va, ça va. A Vespa. We'll get you a Vespa.'

Maman looks up. 'Isn't that dangerous?'

Papa gives the French shoulder shrug. 'Bof! We'll get her a helmet.'

The green man appeared and Dot and I walked past the waiting Vespas and turned left at the petanque sandpit. Men, aged between 50 and 99 years, stood in this pit, smoking. Their skin was so tanned and weathered. These old boys played in their pit for hours, rolling silver balls to try and hit other silver balls. It must have been exciting, cause they were there each day and looked as happy as dusty desert rats.

We continued along the esplanade, past the dude who hires out yellow kayaks by the half hour, and finally took the steps down to the beach, walking over hot pebbles to our spot. Plonking our mats down, we gave the Dream Team a smile and a wave. It was the same four women each day. They were about seventy years old and they wore bikinis, their skin as weathered as the petanque dudes. They played cards at a fold-out table, and smoked and drank vodka. Wearing bikinis and drinking shots at 11 a.m. I nodded respectfully.

The water of Nice Beach goes a chalky blue colour at times. That blue colour, along with the slow rocking movement of the waves, mesmerises and calms me, but the calming sea can be deceptive. One day, I was lying on my foam mat watching the small children playing at the water's edge. Their little Buddha-shaped bodies sat, slapping the water. The sea was moving rhythmically when suddenly a freak wave rose up, like a giant cobra's head. The wave rose high at the shoreline, then slammed down on the children. There was about five seconds of slow-motion silence before shocked adults further up the beach sprang to their feet. They came running past me towards the shore. It looked like an Olympic sprinting event for all ages and body shapes. Mothers, fathers, grandmas, grandads, aunts, and family friends did the ten-yard dash to pluck drenched children out of the sea. The kids looked like stunned rag dolls. The adults, each holding a limp child, looked at each other in bewilderment and suddenly bursting out laughing. The freak wave incident had held just the right amount of fear followed by relief to get everyone giggling for the rest of the day.

The beach had it all going on, the Dream Team, the children, the tourists, and the Cooler Man. The Cooler Man was a stocky older man, about mid-fifties, with old leather skin. He walked barefoot up and down the beach each day, in his swim trunks, balancing a cooler of drinks on his naked shoulder. As he walked he made a noise, which I imagine a yodelling shepherd might make, sort of, 'Eeee-eeee-eeee-ooooo-eeee-uuuuuup!' and people would flock to him.

I noted his cracked bare feet as he carried his cooler the length of the beach. He had probably walked over every single hot pebble on Nice Beach during his lifetime. I don't know how he did it. Miss Dot and I had bought those ridiculously unattractive rubber shoes just so we could walk from our foam mats down to the water.

Dot was good company and a good friend. The problem was that she didn't want to be just "a good friend."

'Here, let me help you with that,' she'd said on our walk to the beach.

'My book?' I'd said, 'you want to carry my book for me?'

'It looks heavy, pass it over.'

'No, I'm good.'

She desperately wanted to do things for me, or buy things for me.

'Where did the cushions come from?' I'd said, looking at the new cushions on the balcony.

'I bought them,' said Dot, taking a seat. 'More comfortable. Do you like them?'

My hand went to the back of my neck. 'Yes.'

'Would you like more coffee? I've made fresh coffee?'

'No, I'm still going on the last one you made, thanks.'

That first night she slept in my sofa-bed, I had let her hold my hand whilst I slid into bed. I had let her hands go to my face. I had caved in for a kiss. Shit fuck poo crap what's wrong with me shit selfish shit jesus grrrrrrr aaaaahhhhhh sheeeeeeeesh.

The very next day I had started scratching my neck of course, and welcomed back confusion and my two internal personalities, although Personality Number Two wasn't confused.

"Just enjoy it, she's only here for six weeks, what's your problem? Someone likes you? That's your problem? Jesus! For fuck's sake!"

Personality Number One was not in agreement. "You hypocrite! You say you want to be mature, yet you cannot even be honest with yourself. Have you had a look at your relationship with alcohol? Why don't you start there?"

"Blah blah blah," said Number Two.

"Be honest!" screamed Number One. "You're not crazy about touching her. But you like being touched, don't you? When you've had some drinks. Can't you see it? Please tell me you can see it!"

"Shut up." Number Two yawned.

"You shut up!" Number One said. "Infantile!"

I started to distance myself from Dot. If she was on the balcony, I stayed in the studio. If she came into the studio, I made an excuse to go out to the balcony. When on the beach, I always took a book. In the evening, I jumped into bed, turning my back to her.

Quickly, she sank into a sulky, depressive mood.

'Let's go for a long walk,' I said one night, in an attempt to lift her from her mood.

Downstairs on the corner, the pizza dog was lying in front of his house.

'Bonsoir dog,' I said.

'Bonsoir dog,' Dot grumbled.

We turned left at the corner. I sniffed the bubbling cheese in the air and peeked inside. All six plastic tables were filled with hungry people talking loudly, even at this late hour. Stephane, the pizza place owner, was working double-speed by the wood fire. We continued past the bakery and the pharmacy, past the mini-mart, and kept going in the direction of Nice centre.

It felt freeing, walking late at night along the streets, wearing a singlet top, skirt and sandals. My arms swung by my sides and I breathed in the smell of hibiscus flowers. My hair was tied up on top of my head and I felt the balmy summer evening air blowing on my crusty neck. My feeling of tranquility got put on hold, however, as we neared a part of the street which was buzzing with people.

'Oh wow,' I said, slowing my steps. My eyebrows raised as high as they would go. 'I walk past here nearly every day. I never knew.'

Dot and I stopped to study the camaraderie of the group on the pavement across the road. One girl, wearing a PVC black skirt and knee-high boots, lit another similarly dressed girl's cigarette. Another girl helped a ladyboy reposition his shiny boob-tube top, whilst another girl, wearing fishnet stockings, talked on her mobile, laughing and flicking her long wig-hair. Cars slowed down, and the ladies and gentlemen of the night sashayed forward to the car windows. Serious business unfolded before us.

My very curious eyes devoured the images of this night market of shi shi and hoo hoo. A smile spread across my face. 'A prostitute community on my doorstep, and I never knew!' I nodded towards the young guys. 'Look at their make-up. It's beautiful!'

One of the boy-girl prostitutes saw me staring. He grabbed his crotch. 'Is this what you're looking for, Madame?' He laughed hysterically.

'Funny you should ask!' I said lightly, chuckling at my own joke, only to look up and see Dot's face. It was white with anger and frustration.

'You don't take us seriously, do you?' she said, hands on her hips.

Inside my head, I rolled my eyes. Outside my head, I sighed and pulled her close, so she would lower her voice. I started to walk her back towards the studio.

My voice was low but firm. 'Because we aren't serious. Try not to expect more of me. I cannot even cope with the idea of being a lesbian. I am paranoid. I don't want my family to know, cause I don't know how I feel,' I said. Internally I added, "and I don't want to be burned on a stake, taken to a priest, or have spells put on me. And and and and and and and and anddddddddddddd....., may I remind you, you were the one who said you would come over just as friends." Number One came bursting into my head, "But you were the one who let her kiss you the first night, so really, you are giving mixed messages."

Number Two said, "So what?"

My lips pressed tightly as I marched along. Dot's eyes cried. When we reached the pizza place, Stephane was by the window handing over pizzas to a customer.

'Bonsoir,' he said, his big smile freezing when he saw Dot's face.

'Bonsoir,' I answered, walking past.

Such a polite country. Even the dog greeted us with a little wag of his tail.

Inside the apartment block, the elevator was out of order. We climbed the stairs in silence, passing the dodgy landlord's place on the fifth floor and finally reaching the sixth.

'Surprise!' yelled two girls, their backpacks leaning against my front door.

'Hallelujah!' Maria-Louisa stretched out her chubby arms. 'We thought ya'd never come!' Her heavy Australian accent rang through the stairwell. She brushed a strand of long black hair away from her eyes, her beautiful smile illuminating her face.

Her skinny travel buddy stood, smoothing her red hair from her pale face. She wore jeans and a singlet top, which hung on her flat chest.

Stretching out her hand, the travel buddy gave me a warm smile. 'Real good to meet you! I'm Kerrie.'

Maria-Louisa moved towards me. 'Didn't Mango tell ya we were coming?'

The text message! I had forgotten.

'Ye, ye, ye, yeeeeees!' I nodded and gave Maria-Louisa a smile. My left arm went around her in a hug, and my right hand went to the back of my neck. Dot was quietly standing behind me. 'This is my friend, Dot. Dot, this is Maria-Louisa, and Kerrie.'

The girls shared smiles and waves hello.

'Come in, come in.' I led the girls through to the studio.

Dot followed, wiping away what I hoped was the last of her tears.

Maria-Louisa went straight to the sliding doors. With no sense of volume control, she shouted, 'Holy Shit! Is that ya view?'

I couldn't help but laugh. 'Yes, a pity it's dark, but you will see in the morning, it's gorgeous,' I said.

'Mind if I use your loo?' asked Kerrie.

I pointed towards the bathroom.

I showed Maria-Louisa the studio with one wave of my hand.

'Voila! The bedroom, lounge room, kitchen, and study!' I twirled around my white-tiled room, decorated with my sofa bed, my desk upon which sat two computers, and my television. 'I'm short on beds, but I've got floor space,' I said.

'That's cool. We are so tired we could sleep anywhere,' Maria-Louisa said in such a loud voice that I began to wonder if she had hearing problems.

She didn't, because the toilet revved into lawnmower sound and her head whipped around.

'Holy Shit! What was that?'

Kerrie's bony body came running out. 'I just pressed the flush button, I'm sorry!'

Dot and I burst out laughing.

On the balcony, I opened a bottle of red, and poured for everyone.

'Cheers!'

The girls' smiles were infectious.

'It's really good to see you again.' I smiled at Maria-Louisa.

'I know, it's been ages,' she said, 'but like I said to Mango, "I'm going to Europe, I better see ya sister while I'm there cause I reckon it's easier seeing her in Europe than it is in Australia!"' She laughed at her own joke, before continuing in her loud voice, 'I'm bloody glad I did, cause,' she waved her arm about her, 'look at where ya live!'

'It's beautiful,' said her sidekick.

An hour later, with my explanations of the loo, the dangerous balcony, and Dot staying as my visiting friend, the girls said they were ready for bed.

'We didn't sleep much last night, cause we had to catch an early train this morning. Sorry, Mica, we'll be more alive tomorrow. Hope ya don't mind?' said Maria-Louisa. Her head tilted apologetically.

They collapsed onto their mats in the corner by the desk. Dot and I silently unfolded the sofa bed. I slowly got into my side of the bed avoiding Dot's eyes. I lay very still, looking at the ceiling for a long time.

In the morning, my Australian guests woke re-energised and went out to the balcony.

'Oh my Gawd!' said loud Maria-Louisa, 'it's so beautiful!' Her perfect smile overtook her face.

Kerrie, dressed in another baggy singlet top and loose long shorts, held a hand to protect her eyes from the sunlight. 'Yeah, I reckon. It's gorgeous!'

I positioned the little balcony table between the two chaises longues and placed a bundle of warm croissants down. Dot carried the coffee out.

'Are you sure you slept okay on the floor, in the corner?' I asked, passing out plates.

'Are ya kidding? I was in heaven,' said Maria-Louisa. She looked around at the balcony. 'I reckon I'm gonna sleep out here tonight though,' she said with a cheeky grin.

Kerrie, sitting next to her, said, 'I was just about to say the same thing! The balcony is the same size as the inside!'

'Yeah!' said Maria-Louisa, 'let's do it! Camping under the stars, that'll be another thing to add to our sleeping stories!'

I looked at her smiling face, waiting for the inevitable story.

'Like in London,' blurted Maria-Louisa excitedly, 'we shared a three-bedroom house with ten people, and Kerrie and I shared a room with a double bed. Yeah, we were lucky to have that. Big Mark slept in the corridor on a bloody baby's mattress!' she said.

'Plus we had Stevo, remember?' Kerrie said.

'Oh yeah, Stevo, slept in the combi van, in our driveway!'

'Eleven. There were eleven of us in the house. One bathroom.'

'It's just like that isn't it, in Europe?' said Maria-Louisa, shrugging her shoulders.

'Is it?' I said.

'Yeah, it's just expensive,' she said.

'Yeah. When we were in Rome, three girls slept in one bed in our hostel. It's just the way it is, hey?' Kerrie added.

My eyes went to Dot, who was sitting quietly with her croissant and blueberry jam.

Maria-Louisa added what would become her catch-phrase over the next two days, 'Yeah. It's not like that in Australia.'

The girls were easy guests.

'What do you want to do?' I asked after breakfast.

'Beach!' They said in unison.

'We've seen so many museums and art galleries,' said Kerrie, 'that for these two days it would be nice to do nothing, you know?' She gave me a genuine smile.

I slapped my knees. 'Beach it is then!'

We went to the beach both days, stopping by the supermarket on the way for lunch food.

Maria-Louisa looked at the cheese section. 'French people must eat cheese non-stop. We don't have this much cheese in Australia. Do we, Kerrie?'

'Nah. We don't have this much cheese,' Kerrie agreed, wrinkling her freckled nose at a blue cheese.

'Oh my Gawd, look at the bread section!' Maria-Louisa led us over to the bread.

Kerrie looked around. 'Where's the normal bread?'

I hesitated, before saying, 'There is some sliced bread by the cake section.'

Maria-Louisa saw a bread slicer sitting by the loaves. 'Ya gotta slice your own bread?'

I nodded. 'Yep, if you want to.'

I hadn't seen many bread-slicers in French supermarkets, and I thought it was a considerate touch, perhaps primarily for the tourists.

Maria-Louisa shook her head. 'Doesn't make sense. Why don't they just slice all the bread and bag it? Like we do, in Australia.'

'Beach?' I said, picking up two baguettes and leading the girls to the tills.

Once at the beach, I proudly led the girls past the Dream Team, to our spot. They looked around with delight.

'Geez, the water's bloody beautiful,' said Kerrie, spreading out her towel.

'Yeah,' agreed Maria-Louisa, laying on her towel. 'Oh my Gawd, these pebbles are uncomfortable. It's not like this in Australia, we've got white sand on our beaches.'

Everyone relaxed. Kerrie started reading her crime novel.

Dot lay with a hat covering her face. I sat, watching two five-year-old boys playing at the shoreline. Maria-Louisa slathered on sunscreen, watching the boys too.

One of the boys, wearing light blue swim shorts, sneakily went and picked up a large rock. Using his little muscles, he balanced his rock carefully on his shoulder, nearly tipping over with the weight. He crept back toward his little unsuspecting friend at the water's edge.

'This little vegemite is getting into some mischief,' said Maria-Louisa, nodding to him.

'Non, Frederic!' A warning came from Maman a little further up the beach.

Frederic ignored Maman. He took a step closer to his curly-haired friend, who had his back to him. He positioned himself and his rock steady, for his attack.

'Non, Frederic! Maman's voice got stronger.

Frederic looked up the beach. He gave Maman an innocent smile, still holding the rock on his shoulder. He turned back and crouched closer to his friend.

Papa got involved. 'Frederic!'

Frederic dropped the rock and shook out his hands. What rock? No rock. He sat down next to his all-too-unaware mate, who was still trying to build a sand-castle out of pebbles.

Maria-Louisa laughed softly. 'Cheeky little vegemite.'

Kerrie looked up from her book and said to Dot, 'Do you know Mica from Australia?'

Dot shot me a glance before responding. 'Nah, I met Mica in London. She was working at the hostel I stayed at.'

Maria-Louisa looked at me. 'That's right. Mango said ya were in London, and I was supposed to meet ya there. But by the time I started travelling, she said ya'd moved to France. She said yav always loved France.'

'Yep,' I said, looking at the sea.

'How long do ya reckon ya'll stay?'

'No plans to go back to London.'

'I meant Australia. Don't ya miss it?' Maria-Louisa said.

I pictured fluoro-lit shopping malls full of sliced white bread and processed cheese, and burning stakes and voodoo dolls.

'No.'

Kerrie turned to Dot. 'But you're going back to Australia, right?'

'Yeah, I've got a few more weeks, then I go back,' said Dot, picking up a pebble and throwing it softly.

'Bet ya looking forward to it, hey?' said Maria-Louisa.

Dot looked out to the sea. 'Yeah and no,' she said. 'I'm going to miss the people.' She lowered her head.

I sent out a silent prayer for no tears.

Dot put on a Matt Damon smile and asked the girls, 'When are you guys going home?'

'I've got six more months back in London to work and save up,' said Kerrie.

'And I go back in three weeks, fly out of London,' said Maria-Louisa. 'Can't bloody wait.'

I gave Dot a warm smile, grateful for her easy-going behaviour in front of the girls.

'Not long now till you're home too, Dot. Cool idea, for you to spend your last weeks lazing around in the South of France,' said Kerrie. 'Perfect way to finish your travels. '

Maria-Louisa laughed. 'Yeah, it's a lot easier when yav got a mate who is living here. Who wouldn't take that opportunity?'

Dot stared down at the pebbles in front of her.

'Bet you're going to miss Dot when she goes, hey?' Kerrie said to me.

My head bowed. 'Mmmmmmmmmm.'

Number One was disgusted. "Good Lord, you can't even say, 'Yes'. Play the damn game. Dot is playing it! Do your part."

'Yes, it's going to be really different when she goes,' I said.

Dot's head whipped around, her eyes were wide with hope. She opened her mouth to speak.

'But,' I added, 'when she goes, it's the end of the holiday period for me, and the beginning of my real life here. I'm really looking forward to that.'

Dot's shoulders slumped, and she turned back to face the beach.

'Yeah, that's true,' said Kerrie, nodding.

'Yeah, can't live the holiday life forever,' said Maria-Louisa.

'No, I can't,' I said, standing. 'I'm going in.'

I walked to the water's edge, where Frederic and his curly-haired friend were playing. I stepped into the magnificent Mediterranean water, sucking in my stomach as I went, adjusting to the water temperature. I looked down through the clear water to see my red-painted toenails. With a deep breath, I took the final plunge, diving in and swimming out as far as I could, feeling my body stretch with each stroke. I floated, rolled, and played in the clear sea for ages.

Eventually, once back in waist-deep water, I stood up. I saw Dot sitting on her mat, holding her camera towards me.

'No!' I shouted to her, wiping the water from my face.

Click!

Dot kept the camera to her eye, ready for another shot.

I shook my head and moved a step closer, about to shout again, but I didn't have time because I got bitch-slapped from behind by a freak cobra wave. It shoved me face first, onto my hands and knees, into the water. White foam swirled around me as I stumbled to stand on the upturned pebbles. All my hair had gone from the back of my head, to all over my face. I raised both arms, pushing long strands from my face.

Dot called out. 'Baby! Are you alright?'

Upon hearing that word, my mouth tightened, and heat raced up my neck. I stood up straight, shoving hair angrily from my face.

Dot looked on anxiously. 'Mica, you...' She started to get up.

I cut her off. 'I'm fine!' I shouted, standing in the swirling water, brushing endless strands of hair from my hot face.

'Okay!' she called, shrugging and relaxing back on her mat. A smile spread over her face.

Maria-Louisa and Kerrie had started laughing. Dot joined them in their laughter.

'Mica!' called Maria-Louisa, 'ya top!' She pointed to my bikini.

I looked down. One of my breasts was exposed. My body was tanned so deeply, except for my breasts and butt, which were fluorescent white. I panicked. I was standing in knee-deep foamy water with my super-white breast exposed, facing The Dream Team, The Cooler Man, the tourists, and Frederic and his mate. A burning wave of humiliation rose over my entire body.

In shock, I saw Dot's body shaking up and down with the giggles, whilst holding her camera to her face.

'Say cheese!' she called. Click! Click! Click!

Chapter 5

It's difficult to escape pizza in Nice. There are restaurants everywhere, plus mobile pizza caravans parked on the streets. Imagine having that conversation.

'Where do you work?'

'On the corner of Avenue St-Marguerite and Boulevard Napoleon III. I'm there every night.'

'Corner? Do you, ah, er, are you...? Every night?'

'Yes. It's good business, good money. It gets very hot in there, that's the only thing.'

'In the?'

'Caravan. People are always hungry.'

'For?'

'Everything. Quatre Fromages, Royale, Margherita, Pescator, Calzone, everything!'

'Ahhhhhhh! I get you. Pizza!'

Each time Dot and I walked past our pizza restaurant on the corner, Stephane was by the take-away window, stretching out dough. He was in his mid-forties, had thick dark hair, and a great happy smile. He always wore white trousers and a white t-shirt, which accentuated his strong tanned arms. Given his locality and what he had to offer, it was inevitable we were going to develop a precious relationship with him.

I loved the Capriciosa and La Reine pizzas, and luckily

Dot loved whatever I loved. We always got two large pizzas, except for the time Dot came back with three. She must have been thinking aloud, and she said, 'Un Capriciosa, and er, er, der, La Reine, s'il vous plait.'

One magnificent sunny day we were walking back to the studio, and just after we'd passed the doghouse, Dot said, 'Stephane's a good-looking guy.'

I nearly gave myself whiplash looking around to her. I beamed a smile and waited for her to say more, but she didn't. Nevertheless, I was delighted at the curveball because the night Maria-Louisa and Kerry left, something had clicked in Dot and she had one hundred percent ramped up her declarations of love. Perhaps it was a combination of being alone again, knowing her departure date was close and me putting my foot down to "just friends" after the Prozzie night. All of it had brought out a certain desperation in her. The evening we said goodbye to the girls, she'd started.

'You know, I can't imagine not being with you.'

My lips had tightened, but I kept my eyes on my computer screen. 'This is a good site for finding other expats,' I said, getting up and taking a bottle of wine out to the balcony.

The next day at the beach, sitting on my green mat, I'd taken a bite of my ham and cheese baguette.

'This is the good ham,' I said, with my mouth full. 'I love this Parma ham.'

Dot looked at me with melting eyes. 'And I love you.'

I took another bite. 'Mmmmmmm. Really good.'

My responses hadn't deterred her. Walking home along the busy promenade, we'd passed an older couple holding hands.

Dot said, 'I'm going to love you forever. There'll never be anyone other than you.'

I pointed to the restaurant coming up. 'We haven't been there yet. We could go for your last night?'

So, this magnificent sunny day, the fact Dot had even noticed Stephane made my heart somersault over and over and over again, circus-style. I heard drum rolls and symbols clashing and I saw myself applauding, "Bravo! More! I want more! I want more! Encore!"

Our personal relationship was on the skids big-time, but our pizza relationship with Stephane was working brilliantly, until August came.

On August 1st, Dot burst into the studio. 'He's gone!'

'Who's gone?'

'Stephane!'

'What do you mean he's gone?'

'He's gone! The pizza place is closed. There's a sign on the door but I can't read it.'

'And the dog?'

'He's gone too!'

I ran downstairs and sure enough, the place was closed

for two weeks.

"Chers patrons, Nous sommes partis à nous bronzer. Nous rouvrons dans deux semaines. Bien à vous, Stephane."

August is the month where lots of businesses pack up and go on holiday, and without any warning to us, Stephane had done just this. We were forced to go to the other pizza place, at the corner, but to the right. Everything we needed at the bottom of our street was to the left; the pizza place, the bakery, the pharmacy, the mini-mart, and the all-you-need shop with the ridiculously unattractive beach shoes. We never turned right.

It was totally different from Stephane's place. It had black tables, black chairs and you couldn't see their wood-fire stove. There was no dog.

'Bonsoir,' a young guy with blond hair greeted us.

'Bonsoir,' we replied in tentative voices. 'Une Capriosa et une Reine, s'il vous plait.'

What happened next was a catastrophe. The last thing we expected was to fall in love with the new pizza. It was the thin crust that did it. It was the most delicious crust for an already delicious pizza. Why didn't Stephane use the thin crust?

Stephane and his dog came back from holiday two weeks later. He opened his takeaway window, ready and refreshed for another year of good business.

'Bonjour!' Stephane waved as we walked past. His happy face was tanned and relaxed. The dog, lying by his bowl of water, gave us a warm tail wag too.

'Bonjour,' we muttered, heads bowed.

I whispered to Dot, 'How are we going to walk past Stephane's place, with a huge pizza box from the other place?'

'We're not.'

'What?' My heart sank.

'I won't do it,' she said. She refused to be seen carrying a pizza box from the competition, past her boyfriend's window.

'Come on. We'll just have to walk really fast,' I said.

'No.'

'I thought you loved the new thin crust.'

'I do.'

'Yeah, but you love your boyfriend more, right?'

Loyal to the bitter end, that's all I needed. I was too deeply in love with the new thin crust. I had to have it.

That night, I defiantly turned right. I made Dot go and stand by Stephane's window, and I went to order at the thin-crust place. From the black tables, I looked out to see Dot keeping watch, and when she nodded to indicate Stephane wasn't anywhere near his window, I bolted to the safety of our front gate. Hurrah! Bon appétit!

Joanne, an Australian friend who I'd met in an Earl's Court pub, came to visit. Joanne had known about Dot but had never met her.

'Nice to meet you,' Joanne stretched out her elegant hand to Dot.

Dot smiled. 'And you.'

Joanne looked around the studio. 'Where is it? I've got to see this lawnmower toilet.'

I pointed. 'When you're finished, come out to the balcony.'

Ten seconds later, I heard the lawnmower, followed by fits of laughter.

On the balcony, with her hands on her waist, Joanne said, 'It is really loud, isn't it?'

'Yes,' laughed Dot, handing Joanne a glass of red wine.

I opened the pizza boxes, Stephane's, Dot wouldn't play the game.

Joanne sat her thin, neat body alongside Dot on the chaise longue. I took the other, opposite them.

'Mica says you're a kindergarten teacher?' Dot said.

'Yes,' answered Joanne. 'And you're a supply teacher? Primary? Secondary?'

'Primary,' said Dot. 'I'm thinking of changing career when I get back to Australia.'

Joanne raised her eyebrows in mock surprise. 'I can't imagine why! Is it the long hours of prep, the spoilt brats, the lack of support from senior staff, the horrible complaining indulgent parents, or the meagre salary? Which one?'

'None, I'm just lazy,' Dot joked.

Joanne laughed, placing her hand on Dot's hand.

'Don't you just love the education system?' Joanne said, picking up her wine glass.

Dot picked up her wine, they clinked glasses and drank. I looked down at my wine glass, still sitting on the little table between us.

The girls continued their tête-a-tête.

'Whereabouts in Australia are you from?' Dot asked.

'A small town in New South Wales.'

'Yeah? What's it called?'

'Narrabri.'

'Narrabri? I'm from Gunnedah!' said Dot.

'No way!' said Joanne, her eyes lighting up. 'We're neighbours!'

Dot reached for her wine glass and they had another clink and cheers. I looked down at my wine glass, still sitting on the table. I reached down for a slice of pizza, and continued watching the dynamic duo. Dot's body was relaxed, and she smiled generously at Joanne. Joanne, in turn, twisted her body more into Dot's and she started flicking her thick hair. She swung a delicate long leg back and forth.

'Oh my God, tell me about Gunnedah. I've been through there so many times.'

Dot happily answered Joanne's non-stop questions, and as the conversation flowed, they found more and more commonalities. They were certainly enjoying each other's company. From my vantage point, as in just opposite them, I could see that Joanne, my good friend, was clearly into Dot. However, knowing Dot as I did, I could see she was simply being friendly. I found my straight friend's attraction to Dot intriguing. And both were acting as if I wasn't even there!

'You're so funny!' Joanne squealed, placing her hand, again, on Dot's hand.

Dot laughed. I frowned. Seriously, wasn't Dot picking up Joanne's signs? Or was I going nuts?

'Tell me more,' said Joanne, her shiny eyes fixed on Dot.

I took another bite of my third Capriciosa slice, and I watched. I mused. I finished the rest of the pizza. I picked up my wine glass, raising it up in a silent cheers to myself.

The next day going into Nice Centre on the rickety old bus, we sat in the four-seater section, on those plastic-type seats that stick to the backs of your legs. Dot and Joanne sat side by side. I sat opposite.

Dot stood and tried to pull the window down, but it was stuck. Sitting back down, she said, 'Jeez, is it hot enough for you?'

Joanne shrieked with laughter. She leant in, both hands on Dot's arm, and gave Dot a peck on the cheek. My eyebrows raised. Dot finally looked uncomfortable. She couldn't have moved any closer to that window if she tried. I tried to keep the smirk off my face. What the hell was going on? It seemed my straight friend was in love with my wannabe-girlfriend, who was totally in love with me, and I was in love with the new thin-crust pizza.

That evening was spent on the balcony sharing a Coq au Vin, prepared by me in my mini oven. I had wanted to make something French for Joanne, to celebrate her last evening, and even though it was very hot weather, Coq au Vin was all I knew how to cook.

There was a lot of movement on the streets below, much more so than usual. People were chanting in groups and they had whistles and horns. From the balcony, we could hear, and feel, a growing excitement. The surrounding apartments came alive too. Usually, I never noticed anyone on their balconies, but this evening, most of the balconies were full of people drinking and cheering.

'What's going on?' asked Joanne, after hearing another group chanting.

'I don't know,' I said, looking down into the darkening streets below, 'but something is going on.''What are they saying?' Joanne asked.

We stopped to listen.

'Something blue,' I said, shrugging.

I looked around at my neighbours. In the apartment across the road, I could see an older woman standing alone on her balcony. It looked like she was wearing curlers in her hair, a summer nightdress, and slippers.

'Something is going on,' I repeated.

It didn't take too much longer for three of us to figure it out. Just as we were finishing the Coq Au Vin, we heard one word, shouted by the neighbourhood.

'Goal!'

Nice city erupted. People jumped up and down, embraced, blew horns and whistles, clashed pots together, cheered, laughed, and sung. It was a rowdy ninety minutes, with lots of 'Goal!', lots of colourful adult words, quite a few 'Ooooooooooh!'s, and some gripping silence. At the end of the game, the victorious people of Nice celebrated in the streets. Car horns beeped non-stop, people chanted, and some people even set off fireworks. Someone from our building shot off a firework in the direction of the old lady, who was still standing on her balcony in her curlers.

My eyes widened. 'God, she's going to get hit!'

Joanne gasped, her hand on her chest. 'What's 911 in French?'

The firework flew past the old lady's head and disappeared into the night.

'Fuck!' we said in unison.

'She didn't move!' I said, shaking my head.

'It nearly got her!' said Dot, stunned.

'Maybe she's blind?' said Joanne.

'Maybe she's the luckiest woman in Nice!' I said, sitting back down. 'God, that was stressful.'

The girls took a seat too, next to each other.

A year later, I was having coffee with Joanne. I gently asked, 'You seemed to really like Dot?'

'I did. I loved the way she loved you. I've always wanted someone to love me like that.'

Always the case, isn't it? What we don't want, someone else will. I could have sworn she was hitting on Dot, but in fact, she was attracted to her devotion and personality. As was I, but I wasn't playing fair.

After Joanne left, my psoriasis got itchier. I needed to release stress. 'Going for a run,' I said, picking up my MP3.

I made my way towards the promenade. Stevie Wonder's 'Superstition' rang through my earphones. I jogged past the petanque Desert Rats and along the promenade, past the kayak dude.

Trying hard not to overthink things with Dot, I focussed on the here and now. I asked myself, 'What can I see, right here, right now?' Cloudless blue sky, white railings, white benches, tanned and glamorous older lady walking towards me, her partner, equally tanned and dressed in white. As I jogged past the woman, I got hit with a waft of Hermes 24 Faubourg. 'What else?' A balding, middle-aged, white man with an enormous belly. He was wearing flip-flops, a backpack, and tiny speedos, hardly visible because of his impressive stomach. Weirdly, it was the backpack that looked out of place. 'Try A Little Tenderness' came on. I continued jogging and went past our spot on the beach. When I reached the Hotel Negresco I stopped to admire the grand building with its dome and pastel colours. I faced the seafront as 'The Gambler' came on, and took a seat on a bench.

Two older boys played near the shoreline, chasing each other. One accidentally hit the other on his cheek. He said sorry, leant in and kissed his friend's cheek. They both laughed. So did I. I loved that two 14-year-old boys could play like that, and imitate their mothers, or fathers, kissing something better. France is a country where you kiss to say hello, goodbye, and in this case, to make something better. There was zero sexual connotation about that gesture. There was no reaction, like, "What are you, gay?" or pushing the other away.

I glanced up and nodded hello to a greasy-haired man in his early forties, who had come to share my bench. As he sat, his eyes travelled down to my lycra-clad thighs. I turned my head back to the beach and looked at the 14 year olds. I asked myself why this particular scene spoke to me. Why did I think, "That's good, it didn't even occur to them to think of it as gay"? Something deep inside niggled me, and it had nothing to do with being straight or gay, nothing to do with Dot and her declarations, and everything to do with me and the amount of energy I spent on what others thought. It dawned on me that this was possibly a technique I used to keep me from the real issue. The real issue was my beliefs about men and relationships. I knew I was attracted to men. Perhaps it was time to address my avoidance of them.

'Bonjour,' said greasy hair, to my left. His hungry eyes invited me to his grotty bed.

Right this second was not the time, but I knew I would have to address the issue soon.

Chapter 6

The stationery shop displayed a tiger, made entirely of pink paper roses, in its window. White paper flowers lay scattered on the floor, plus a quill pen, a dark leather diary, and an open box of fancy envelopes. My eyes travelled up and down the tiger standing on its hind legs, admiring the beauty.

'Il est beau, non?' said a familiar voice.

Michelle was a friend of a friend from Streatham. We had met a year ago when she moved to London. She was back in her native Nice for a flying visit. It was so exciting to see someone I knew, from the UK, in Nice. We went to a cafe, and I took the opportunity to drill her on her insider knowledge.

'Okay,' she said, nodding at my question, 'there's a good restaurant on the other side of the port. All they do are mussels, with frites. You can eat as many as you like! They do refillable plates.'

'Refillable plates of mussels?'

'Yes!'

'All you can eat?'

'Yes!' She laughed at my surprised face.

Nice Port has its share of sparkling bling-bling-bling millionaire yachts docked in the port. Young dudes, wearing navy polo shirts and tan shorts, polish each opulent inch of these yachts. At the same time, older bronzed dudes wearing more expensive navy polo shirts, white shorts, and designer sunglasses, talk on mobile phones. Thin women, wearing over-sized floppy hats, over-sized designer sunglasses, and under-sized skirts, are helped onboard by the younger dudes.

These enormous yachts with the latest technology are the crème-de-la-créme. They are pure mobile luxury, the Smooth Operators. On the other side of the port, are the Ready-to-go-to-work Operators. These are the colourful fishermen rowing boats, which are lined up, one after the after. It is past these rowing boats that we found the mussels restaurant.

'Bonsoir.' A waitress greeted us.

'Bonsoir.'

'A table for two?' Having heard our accents, she switched to English.

'Oui,' I said, annoyed she had switched to English.

'Inside or out?' she asked, gesturing to the little tables on the footpath.

'Ici, c'est parfait.' I pointed to the footpath.

'Please, have a seat, I come with menus.' She took her tiny little body back inside the restaurant.

We sat on the terrace, across the road from the pink, blue, and green rowing boats. On the other side of the port, the millionaire super yachts were sparkling under the sun, even though it was seven-thirty at night.

Our mussels in white wine sauce arrived piping hot in a big old pot that looked so old it could have belonged in my grandmother's kitchen.

'You first.' I handed Dot the serving spoon. Before I even put a mussel in my mouth, I knew they would be good because the white wine smell was making my eyes roll to the back of my head.

'Bon appétit!'

'Bon appétit!'

The combination of wine, fries, mussels, blue skies, clear waters, diamond yachts, and coloured rowing boats was the 'Bingo!' jackpot.

We visited the mussels restaurant two more times that week, cycling along the long esplanade to reach the restaurant. I loved cycling along the sea in the evenings. I felt almost French, cycling in high-heeled sandals, red lipstick, with my black curls swept up in a ponytail. The last time I cycled back from the restaurant however, I had a bad feeling in my stomach and it wasn't from the food. It came from not being able to communicate my feelings to Dot. I had decided my personal issues with men had nothing to do with her, and that she would be leaving very soon, and I would simply wait it out. But soon is eternal when things keep pissing you off.

A number of silly things annoyed me, really little things, like the etiquette of bike-riding. I believe one should ride in single file along the promenade. Dot, however, liked to ride side by side. When she rode up alongside me, I pulled back and fell into single file behind her. Then she pulled back until we were side by side again. So I moved forward.

I was always leading. I'm a naturally bossy person and I

like leading, but not all the time. We were having too many of these conversations:

Me: 'What do you want for dinner?'

Dot: 'I don't mind. What do you feel like?'

Me: 'Where should we go on Sunday?'

Dot: 'I don't mind. Where do you want to go?'

I wanted to make friends in Nice, aware that Dot would be leaving.

'Do you fancy going to an expat night at a pub?' I asked.

'Not really.'

Where was the, "I don't mind," now? Hmmm.

In her last days, Dot finally agreed to go to an expat outing with me. I'd found a group on the web. They meet once a month.

'We're going to a lake, inland somewhere,' I said.

'Okay,' said Ms I-don't-care.

'We have to get to Cannes La Boca train station by 9 a.m.'

'Okay,' said Ms Don't-give-two-hoots.

'Then we all share cars to this lake.'

'Okay,' said Ms I'm-only-doing-this-for-you.

'We'll get into a stranger's car and go to a lake we've never been to before.'

'Okay,' said Ms Why-can't-you-love-me-like-I-love-you.

We arrived at the train station, and were welcomed by a lovely group.

'You two come with me,' said an older English guy, wearing camel-coloured trousers.

We drove inland to the lake.

The scenery was a complete contrast to the bright colours and manicured-ness of the Riviera. The lake was untouched and circled by weeds and rock, and the water was a green-brown colour. The surrounding area was savage too, with wild grass, rocky terrain, and brushy trees. A handful of family groups sat around the lake.

'Right then. Under this tree?' asked one of the women in our group, as we walked to a flat patch.

'Yes, perfect.'

We laid our picnic blankets down and set out the food.

A woman in a Laura Ashley skirt took control. She waved to the food. 'Please help yourselves. There's houmous I made, some chickpea balls, this is a tapenade I got at the market. What else have we got? Oh, we've got ham, and what is this?' She picked up a plate and inspected it. 'Oh, it's quiche, vegetarian by the looks of it, and well, all this other stuff. Everyone help themselves. It's got to be eaten!' She shot me a grin.

'Thanks,' I said, offering our plate of paté mini-toasts and cheese to the picnic.

The group was very welcoming. Most of them knew each

other from previous outings. I watched Gareth, the man who had given us a lift, try to get the attention of Laura Ashley. I had noticed that he had noticed her, all morning. He sat on his blanket, in his camel-coloured trousers, and straightened himself.

'Helen, the melons in Antibes market are rather good this time of year.'

Oooooooooh, I enjoyed listening to him speak. He had a posh accent, very "rah rah yah".

'Oh yes?' murmured Helen. She was busy looking through the box of cutlery.

'Uhm, yes. It's so good that market, isn't it?' said Gareth, trying to make eye contact.

'Hmmmmm, pardon?' Helen shook the cutlery box, looking closer into it.

'The market in Antibes. It's quite varied.'

'I could have sworn I put it in here somewhere.' Helen fished around in the box.

Number Two looked on, smirking. "Dude, Helen isn't interested."

There was a younger guy in the group. He was tall, solidly built, and had a nervous look to him. He stared without blinking when talking to you.

'You live in Nice, do you?' he asked. 'I live in Nice too. Whereabouts in Nice do you live?'

He stared without smiling or blinking.

'Oh, just back from the promenade,' I said.

'Me too. Exactly, where do you live?' He leant closer.

'Fancy a swim, Dot?' I said.

'It's really hot,' she said, jumping to her feet.

I waded waist-deep into the lake water. The sand under my feet, which couldn't be seen through the murky water, was soft. The water was soft too. After months of swimming in saltwater, this lake water seemed unreal, almost sensual. It was like swimming in rippling sheets of satin. I swam out to the centre and looked around me. The luxurious feeling of the water contrasted with its murky colour, and the harsh, rocky surroundings. I let my body float, appreciating the novel experience.

A young couple on horseback slowly rode their magnificent horses into the lake. The girl wore a bikini with her long hair loose, and the guy wore board shorts. They guided the horses into the lake, close to where Dot and I were. I smiled. My eyes took in the strength of the horses' bodies as they glided into the water. I sighed deeply. There was something so real and honest about this experience. It was so far removed from the polished services of the ritzy Riviera, yet geographically so close. The horses topped it off for me, they were beautiful. I was in a dream-like state, filling up on all my senses.

It would have been a perfect ending to the day had I returned to my studio with the strong-looking guy on the white horse, and had he thrown me on the sofa-bed, taken my clothes off, and slowly devoured every inch of my body. Instead, I went back to the studio with my possessive non-girlfriend, who was very relieved to have me back all to herself.

Dot moved towards me in the kitchen, trying to corner me. I poured myself an enormous glass of red wine and ducked out of her attempted embrace. She sighed. I went out to the balcony, seeking room to breathe. It wasn't the right end to a good day and we both knew it. This relationship had become a waiting game, waiting for five more days, and then it was finished, for good.

Previously if I was in a situation I didn't like, I would move. I have moved countries to avoid dealing with things.

'I'm moving to London,' I'd said to my Brisbane friends, after an argument with my mother.

'What? When?' asked my surprised friends.

'Tomorrow.'

This became a pattern in my life. A conflict would enter my world and I would react by moving house, and if not house, then city, if not city, then country. For fifteen years. It's an expensive way of not dealing with issues. In this case though, I was so very happy with my motor toilet and rusty balcony railings, that I wasn't prepared to move. I'd decided to wait it out. Meanwhile, the resentment grew, and I still hadn't learnt to communicate.

Number One was so disappointed. "Really? Would it kill you to open your mouth and say, 'You know what? I've been a bit selfish here. What I really wanted was support, not a physical relationship with you.'"

'And if she starts to cry?' I asked.

Number One said, "You just say, 'Please don't cry. Crying

only adds to my confusion because I do have feelings for you, just not the physical feelings you want me to have. Stop crying.'"

Number Two looked on. "Yeah, right."

I stood on the balcony, nursing a huge glass of wine, staring emptily into blue waters, whilst scratching a new patch of psoriasis on my left forearm.

The next morning, Dot grabbed her wallet and said, 'I'm going out.'

'Okay.'

I could tell by the tone of her voice that she was going to be gone for a while. I stood in the middle of the studio and spread out my arms and twirled in a circle. Skipping over to the kitchen bench, I grabbed my coffee and my croissant, turned on the television and lazed on the sofa, stretching my legs out over the whole sofa.

Dot returned in the late afternoon and stood in the doorway.

I gasped. 'Oh my God, your hair!' I walked over to touch her new bleach-blonde hair. It was short, with a cute little fringe. 'It's so... white!'

Dot laughed. 'I needed a change,' she said with a shrug.

The haircut and colour changed her look completely.

'It suits you,' I said, circling her.

'Thanks,' she said. 'Do you want to go for a swim?'

'Sure.'

Fifteen minutes later, I watched her dive into the clear waters. I followed. When we resurfaced, I saw her shake her short-haired head around. Her triumphant smile told me she had no regrets.

My hair is important to me. You cannot imagine how very important my hair is to me. "You've got great hair," is a compliment I never tire of hearing. I don't think any girl does. It has taken me years to get my hair to a stage where I love it and I can manage it. It's long and straight, when I straighten it, much like it was when I was thirteen.

As a child, I never went to the hairdresser. My Central American mother always cut my hair, outside in the back yard, at midnight, under a crescent moon.

'This way it'll grow back healthier and shinier,' she said, cutting away.

This was one of her "things she does." I didn't question it. Much like I didn't question it when she caught one of the chickens in our back yard, took an axe, chopped its head off, and hung it upside down on our washing line for the blood to run out. I developed an attitude of, "Oh, that's just Mum." I took her with a pinch of salt though, because some of the things she said were too much for my teenage suburban Australian brain.

Watching me pile clothes into the washing machine one afternoon, Mum said, 'You're lucky. We had to do our washing in the river.'

I looked at her with my head tilted and my lips pressed together. I kept my mouth shut.

Another time, she watched me peel hard-boiled eggs at

the kitchen sink.

'We had to go down to the beach and dig for our eggs,' she said, 'turtle eggs.'

I looked at her with my head tilted and my lips pressed together. I kept my mouth shut.

In the garden after school one day, she said, 'I saw you talking to that boy from down the road. Watch out. You'll be cursed and get snakes growing in your stomach.'

I looked at her with my head tilted and my lips pressed together. I kept my mouth shut.

I accepted all her "things she does and says" without question, so the first time she said, 'Come and sit under the moon. It's time to cut your hair,' I just picked up a chair and went and sat outside, under the moon. I knew all the other girls went to the hairdressers though, in the daytime.

When I was 14 years old, my mother went to Sydney for a few days, leaving my older sister in charge. 'Come with me,' Mango said as soon as my mother left. 'I'm taking you to the hairdressers.'

I gasped. 'What!?'

Mango smiled from ear to ear. 'Yes. The hairdressers!'

Linking arms, we giggled as we hurried down the road to the train station.

I walked into the local hairdresser salon with thick long hair down to my waist.

'Hello, we have an appointment,' said Mango, pushing me

forward.

I nodded excitedly, too nervous to speak. My eyes scanned the room and took in the mirrors, the swivel chairs, the magazines, and the washbasins at the back. It was heaven, and Duran Duran was playing as the background music. It was so perfect.

The hairdresser stood before me. She was about 25 years old. She was the trendiest person I had ever seen in real life. She was wearing white jeans and a white top, with white high-heeled sandals. Her short blonde hair was permed to perfection and she wore make-up, lots of it. In my eyes, she was a living angel. Her blue eye-shadowed eyes smiled at me.

'Do you want to take a seat?' she gestured to a swivel chair.

I walked past the angel and a perfume I would later recognise as Poison by Dior followed me, starting a life-long obsession.

Placing a large white cape around my shoulders, the angel said, 'And what are we having done today?'

I looked at Mango standing at the front of the salon. 'Cut it all off,' said Mango.

I smiled, hardly able to breathe in my swivel chair.

Forty-five minutes later, I looked in the mirror at my new shoulder-length frizzy rizzy afro.

'Well, well, well!' exclaimed the pretty angel. 'Look at how curly your hair is!'

I grinned like the Cheshire cat, turning my afro from left to right.

'The weight of your hair made it straight, but in actual fact, it's really curly,' said the angel, lifting my curls in her hands.

I smiled with happiness and Cyndi Lauper sang 'Girls Just Want To Have Fun' in the background. Cyndi Lauper and I were in sync!

My mother wasn't grinning when she got back from Sydney. For once though, I didn't care how loudly she screamed. Michael Jackson was in fashion at the time, he had an afro and now so did I.

The afro wasn't to last sadly, for it wasn't long before I learnt the power of the straight blow-dry. I had seen the angel do it to another customer. The first time I straightened my own hair, I had to look twice in the mirror. I turned my head from side to side, with a growing smile.

'So smooth,' I'd said to myself, 'so shiny, so polished, so neat.' I stared at myself in the mirror, astounded at the difference in appearance. I looked more grown-up and sophisticated.

I looked at the hot hairdryer in my hand. 'Yes.' I said to it. 'Yes.'

From then on, I was a devout straightener and my relationship with my hairdryer became, and remains, the priority in my life.

Living in Nice and swimming every day however, it was not practical to have straight hair, so I wasn't the only one who had to get used to looking at a new hairstyle. Dot had had to get used to me, with wild, curly hair. We had both changed physically. Firstly, we had both put on a good amount of weight thanks to the croissants, pizzas, and wine. I loved every part of that. Secondly, I had gone ridiculously brown. So brown that when we walked into the all-you-need shop, the shop assistant looked at me and said, 'You live here.' He looked at Dot and said, 'You don't.'

I thought, "You said it, Man."

Finally, our hairstyles had changed. We were physically different from when we'd first met and the relationship was different. It was in fact, no longer.

The relationship was truly over the day at the beach, with the man. I was swimming in my amazing Nice water when I looked up to see a tall older man get up from his towel and walk over to Dot. They spoke. He walked back, got his things, and walked off.

When I got out of the water later on, I asked, 'What did the man want?'

'He wanted to know if I could look after his things, so he could go to the Cooler Man.'

I looked over at the empty place where he had been. 'And?'

'I pretended that I didn't understand him.'

I sank down onto my mat and stared at the sea. I looked back up the beach towards the Cooler Man.

'Eeee-eeee-eeee-ooooo-eeee-uuuuuup!'

I turned back and stared silently at the sea, taking slow, deep breaths.

In the evening, Dot didn't blink an eyelid at my cold behaviour.

'Do you want to watch that dancing show?' Dot asked, turning on the television.

'Whatever,' I said.

'Mini-mart chicken for dinner?'

'Whatever.'

Now who was being bland and gutless?

Number One came out. "Open your mouth for once, and tell her how you feel, like an adult!"

Number Two said, "She's leaving. Forget it."

Number One was unimpressed. "Wow, you're amazingly gutless. Gut-less. No guts."

I sighed and put my hand on my stomach. I had held so much in internally that I might in fact get snakes in my stomach after all. Three more days. Then, it would definitely be over.

Chapter 7

The Gorge du Verdon, inland from Nice, is ideal for hiking, kayaking, rafting, and rock-climbing. Dot and I stayed in a campsite near the rivers, a surprise last-minute decision, to celebrate her final weekend. I say 'celebrate', perhaps not her choice of word.

The campsite was run by a guy called Laurent. He had sandy blond floppy hair, and an athletic body. He was in his mid-thirties, and wore a t-shirt, loose shorts, and trainers. I was instantly attracted.

'Bonjour.' He ran his hand through his hair, as he welcomed us at reception.

'Bonjour.' I flashed him one of my best smiles.

Number Two jumped on it. "Hey, hey, hey! What's going on here?!"

'Here are your keys,' said Laurent, his lovely green eyes sparkling as he gave me the yellow key ring. 'If you have any questions, you know where to find me.'

Number Two danced with mischief. "Indeed, indeed!"

Outside our caravan, I looked around in joy at the campsite. Once again, I found myself in a contrasted environment to the polished Riviera lifestyle, and I loved it. Caravans and cabins were spread amongst tall leafy trees, on crude rocky grounds. Each caravan and cabin was far enough away from the other, so we all had some privacy. Our caravan had a flimsy front door that didn't look like it would lock properly.

At the communal washing area that evening, I read the sign, "Veuillez s'il vous plait ne pas faire de bruit après 22h jusqu'à 8h du matin."

I happily followed the camp etiquette of respecting noise levels. I find France, on the whole, to be a polite country. It is formal and people conform. It's one of the things that attracts me to her. I grew up with a very loud, non-conforming, moon-worshiping Central American mother. We would have been the family at the campsite who played their music too loud and too late. My mother would have been laughing too loudly, singing with gusto, and swearing without shame. The people in the next caravan wouldn't have minded, as her joie de vivre was infectious, but some of the campsite would have.

'Madame, please be quiet!' they might have said.

A red flag to a bull, I'm afraid. Up the music would have gone and the people in the next caravan would have giggled cheekily, only further encouraging my headstrong mother.

Later in life, when my sister Mango had kids, I babysat them a lot and with big innocent eyes, they would report to me what my mother had been up to.

'And then Nana screamed so loudly that everyone turned to look at us. They said, "shush" like that,' my niece held her finger over her mouth, 'and then Nana shouted even loudlier at them.'

My other niece added, 'And then the man came over and we got into trouble.'

I seemed to spend my teenage years sighing and saying,

'Yes. Nana's very naughty.'

My mischievous mad mother had died by this time in my life, both my parents had. I knew though, that had my mother been alive and found out I was in a 'gay' relationship (whatever you want to call it), that it would have secretly made her laugh. I wasn't totally naïve though. I knew that once the initial delight of me doing something against the grain was over, she would have called the priest, and her sister, Lydia, the spell-maker.

I was very much a good girl growing up, and my mother longed for a rebel daughter. When I was 16, she found a lighter in my underwear drawer, tucked behind my far too large, cotton, olive underpants.

She ambushed me in my room. 'What's this?' She waved the lighter in the air like it was a secret weapon.

Thinking on my feet, 'It's Angela Brown's,' I said, blaming my best friend.

'Ah,' she said, putting the lighter back in its place, and walking out, disappointed.

My mother and her friends used to have amazing parties in the downstairs area of our house when I was young. The parties were filled with her Spanish, Greek and Italian friends. The men wore sideburns and flared trousers, and the women wore short a-line dresses. Everyone passed around vodka jellies and danced to Nana Mouskouri, Harry Belafonte, and Bee Gees music. They drank, talked, laughed, and smoked long into the night. The kids were always asleep long before the evening finished. If the party was at someone else's house, my brother and I would crawl into the back of our car and go to sleep. All the kids did. We each slept in our respective cars, outside in the street, whilst the adults partied inside, safe and sound.

Dot and I signed up for body-surfing down the river rapids. We met the other clients, in the camp carpark, opposite the swimming pool.

'Bonjour!' A thin, bald man waved his hand to us, pulling up in his run-down mini-van. Jumping out of the van, he smiled. 'My name is Yves. I am your guide. Today you do as I say, always, yes?' He looked at us for agreement. 'Other days, you do as you want,' he added, smiling at his joke. Yves clapped his hands. 'Are you ready for excitement?'

I nodded along with the other clients.

'So, please, we get in!' Yves pointed to the mini-van.

Yves drove us away from the campsite and high up the mountain along windy, rocky paths. We bumped up and down till we reached the top, where Yves swung the van around to a stop, and we tumbled out onto the uneven ground.

'Put these on,' said bald Yves, handing out wetsuits and helmets, 'and follow me.'

Yves guided us through the trees as rays of sunshine pushed through the foliage to a river edge. Like penguins in a single file, we followed him into the icy water. Dot and I exchanged smiles as we half-swam, half floated, head-first down the shallow waters. So shallow was the water in this part of the river that my stomach touched the rock bed of the river. I pushed myself using my arms, looking around as I travelled. Blue skies were above, and tall green trees lined both sides of our river. Our group swam along on our stomachs, for about ten minutes, carried by the strong current, till we slowed down behind Yves in deeper waters.

'To the left, okay? We stop,' Yves shouted.

One by one, we veered off to the left-hand side to meet with Yves, who was waiting for us on shore. He led us along the side of the river, to a huge boulder. We followed him, scrambling high up onto the boulder, grabbing at crevices where we could pull ourselves up. Our group assembled on the top of the large boulder, smiling at this surprise element of our river rafting experience. We straightened ourselves and looked down below to the river rapids below.

Pointing down, Yves said, 'Jump!'

I frowned and looked at Dot. No-one had said anything about jumping off rocks.

'Allez! Go!' said Yves to the first guy.

The guy jumped right over the side of the rock, down into the icy-cold rapids. I frowned some more. Our happy group moved forward one by one.

'Go!' said Yves, smiling to the next person in line.

I'm scared of heights. It might be because of my mother and her role in my Brisbane Exhibition experience.

Brisbane has an annual funfair. It's called the Exhibition but the locals call it, "The Ekka." There are lots of cows, bulls, sheep, rides, and lots of food like hot dogs, candy floss, and toffee apples. Everyone gets excited about it.

(Insert broad Australian accent) 'Are ya's goin' to the Ekka?'

'I reckon.'

'Bewdy. See ya's there!'

Every year when we arrived at the Ekka, Mum, my brother and I would go straight to the pub's beer garden to meet my mother's friends. My brother and I would be given money and we would race off to entertain ourselves all day. First stop was always the Dagwood Dog Caravan.

Beebee and I sat on the dusty dirt ground, opened our little sachets of tomato sauce, piled it on our Dagwood Dogs, and bit in. There was so much batter, not a lot of sausage. Perfect for my child palate. A little boy stopped when he saw me eating my Dagwood Dog. His little blond head turned around, searching for it.

'Dagwood Dog!' he shouted, pointing to the van. 'I want one! Please!'

His father dragged him in the opposite direction.

'Cows, bulls, horses, then check-in,' said my brother, swallowing his last mouthful of Dagwood Dog batter.

He led me across the fair-grounds, towards the smelly animal section.

'What about the strawberry ice-cream?' I said, my tongue hanging out of my mouth, trying to lick the last bit of tomato sauce.

'We just had the Dagwood Dog.'

'What about a Toffee Apple?'

'We just had the Dagwood Dog.'

I followed Beebee calmy, because I knew that by the end of the day, I would have a strawberry and vanilla ice-cream, the one with the swirl of cream and a real strawberry on top. I also knew I would have a toffee apple. I didn't know I would become one, one day.

My brother led me into an enormous barn filled with prize cows and bulls.

I pinched my nose. 'Holy Moses!' I said, trying not to breathe in.

I spent the entire visit, looking mostly at the floor, trying to avoid poop.

'Poop!' I pointed to the floor, stepping around it, holding my nose.

My brother ignored me and led me down the aisles, through the barn, stopping to stare at bulls or cows from time to time. I stayed in the aisles, out of the way of heavy hooves, horns, and slobbery wet noses.

Just before the exit was my favourite part. I took my hand away from my nose, and knelt down next to the gate of the baby animal area to pat an inquisitive goat. He had really little horns growing out of his head. His head felt rock hard under my fingers. I knocked on it. My brother found a fluffy rabbit to pat. We took turns with the other kids to pat all the animals, including the Shetland Pony, which stood so patiently while little hands petted and stroked his black mane.

Back outside, I breathed the air deeply. 'Where now?' I asked my brother.

He looked at his watch. 'Come on, we've got to check in.'

Back at the pub, my brother and I exchanged nervous glances. Mother had decided she wanted to come with us on the rides. My mother had an extremely good set of lungs. On a ride, you can scream as loud as you like. On a ride, it was carte blanche for her to let loose. So we went, and she did scream and let loose. She whooped and laughed as we rode The Sizzler, being flung forwards, backwards, upside down, and back again. We ricocheted around and Beebee's white knuckles gripped to the bar at his end, my white knuckles gripped to the bar at my end, and my mother, sitting in the middle, waved her hands high in the air, letting her wild black hair fly about.

'Wooooooooo-hooooooo!'

Later, she wanted to go on the Ferris Wheel. Why, I don't know. The Ferris Wheel is a big, slow-moving ride, so that people can enjoy the view of the fair. The Ferris Wheel is for very young children and patient adults, not for us.

My mother sat next to me in our cage, and my brother sat opposite. We gently made our way higher into the air. Beebee and I gazed down at the doll-like people below. My mother started rocking the carriage with her body.

'Mum, what are you doing?' asked my brother, holding onto the side.

I gripped on to the steel bars close to me, knowing not to say a word, that would only encourage her.

'Yep- pah!' whooped my mother, laughing as she tried to get the carriage swinging.

Now, I can't prove it, but I think it's from that Ekka Ferris Wheel episode that I got my fear of heights.

Yves, our rapid river guide smiled at the 10-year-old boy in the queue. The boy didn't even need to be told to jump, he threw himself off the side, clicking his heels together in the air as he went, like he was bloody Mary Poppins.

The guide smiled at me. 'Jump!' he said, giving me such a forceful push on the shoulder that over I went.

Next to follow was Dot. It happened so unexpectedly and so quickly, that before we knew it, we were in the water again, being swept along by the rapids.

We followed the rapids down through the gorge, in a single file, as the river became more narrow and more shallow. Despite the low level of water, the current was strong. It pulled you at speed, and I thanked goodness for the wetsuit and helmet, as I was constantly crashing into the side of the gorge and its rocks. I looked around to see if anyone else was as stunned as I was, but the rest were smiling and laughing, as if it was a walk in the park. Yves pointed out things of interest as we crawled and swam along. I didn't have time to look around, I simply tried to keep up.

'Coming up, just past that tree sticking into the water,' shouted Yves, 'we stop.'

We pulled into the side. Our soaked and dripping bodies climbed out of the icy water, back onto firm ground.

'Follow me,' said Yves, taking us along the side of the river, till we reached a cliff with a dark tunnel. 'There is no light in here,' he told us.

We looked at each other and kept following him in.

'If you like, you can take your helmet off, and hold it against the side of the tunnel. This will guide you along,' he said.

I took off my helmet and held it to the wall of the tunnel. I smiled, although no-one could see because we were walking, single-file, in pitch-black darkness. It took me a minute to relax and trust my feet were on firm ground, and to step more and more confidently. When I relaxed, with a new appreciation for my helmet, I smiled more. We didn't know where we were heading in this surprise tunnel. The experience was very James Bond, and I loved it.

The rapid river day was so invigorating and stimulating. I should have gone back to the camp-site, grabbed Laurent from reception, and taken him to my caravan. We should have shared a hot camp meal, like Beef Goulash with good French bread and red wine. Then we should have kissed passionately, outdoorsy-rough style, tumbled onto the fragile caravan bed, and had rapid river sex all night.

"How very Barbara Taylor-Bradford," murmured Number Two.

In reality, I went back to the campsite with Dot and we enjoyed a camp dinner of hotdogs, and laughed over the day's events, agreeing it was loads of fun. Still, not so shabby, can't complain. Dot was a good friend and easy to be with, when she wasn't in girlfriend mode.

'Au revoir, Laurent!' I waved, and flashed Laurent my best smile, as we drove away the next day.

His floppy hair and he waved back.

I turned back in my seat and looked to Dot, who was driving. 'Well, that was your last weekend in France!'

Later that day, I watched Dot slowly packing her bags. She rolled her favourite shorts and placed them in her backpack. She would be sitting on her flight, in under 24 hours.

'The Great Pretender' was playing on the radio. I felt pangs of guilt.

'We have similar senses of humour,' I said to Dot, trying to figure out, aloud, how we got to this point.

She nodded without looking at me. She picked up her swimmers and shoved them down a little pocket of her backpack.

I said brightly, 'We can talk about everyday things.'

She picked up her trainers and put them in. She nodded and sighed. I was failing to communicate what I wanted to say.

'We're friends,' I said, my tone more forceful.

She stopped packing and looked at me. 'I love you,' she said, with sad eyes.

I pressed my lips together. Not quite the answer I was expecting. I could hear the rest of the silent sentence, it said, "So, this isn't over."

I walked over to the kitchen, muttering, 'Where is that bottle opener?'

She spent the rest of the afternoon packing, and I spent it on the balcony. In the evening, we took a walk to the mini-mart and picked up a roasted chicken with potatoes to have on the balcony.

'Sure you don't want to eat out?' I asked, walking back to the studio.

She shook her head.

'I'm going to take a long shower,' she said after dinner.

'Cool,' I said, 'I'm going to check my emails.'

I was engrossed in the web when she finally emerged. I had found a site for English Teachers, and was busy reading the Jobs Offered section.

'I'm going to bed,' she said, unfolding the sofa.

'Goodnight,' I said, my eyes glued to the computer.

The next morning, I slowly opened my eyes to a sunny day. I smiled at the ceiling because I knew exactly what today was. I jumped out of bed, leaving Dot to stir next to me. I looked out past the balcony to the airport. I think I had been unconsciously looking at the airport each day for the past month, just imagining today. Now here it was. This time, we both knew it was over. Well, I knew, and the fact that I was one hundred percent certain this time made it impossible for her to break through any weak leak. I was rock solid sure. I put the coffee on, and skipped downstairs to get the croissants. We ate breakfast on the balcony.

I cleared the plates away, swept the floor, then said, 'Oh, look at the time!'

Dot gathered her luggage with less energy than a slug.

I had enough energy for the both of us. My voice was crisp. 'Passport?'

'Got it.' She patted her pocket.

'Ticket?'

'Got it.' She patted the pocket again.

'Good, let's go!' I picked up her little daypack and walked out the studio, leaving her to follow me with her bulky backpack.

In the busy airport terminal, friends and families cried, hugged and fussed over each other. Mothers smoothed down grown sons' shirts, fathers carried daughters' suitcases and lovers linked arms in the check-in queue. The two lovers in front of us stood, locked at the hips, eyes boring into each other. I shuffled beside Dot and gave her a cheeky punch on the arm.

The queue is the place where you can legitimately eavesdrop and study people. In our queue we had the usual suspects. There were the newly together couples, they were the ones who looked at each other every five seconds and regularly made physical contact, a hand on the elbow or a hand on the back. There were the well-travelled older business-class couples. They were the ones where the man looked impatient whilst carrying their Gucci luggage, and the woman looked immaculate by his side, casually dressed in a designer trouser suit, her hair freshly coiffed from the salon. Then there were the age-difference couples. They were the ones where the woman was at least thirty years younger than he was. I know the reverse exists, I just ain't never seen it.

Singles were in the queue too, silently checking their passport and ticket as they pushed their bags along the slow-moving queue. But who knew? Perhaps they weren't single and had just left their lover or partner behind? Who knows what is going on in other people's lives? We can't really tell what is going on with a person or a couple, by what we see with our eyes, can we? I wondered what people were thinking about Dot and me? Shoving the thought out of my head, I looked around and smiled at the baby in the pram behind me. He appreciated my exaggerated smile by giving me a beaming toothless smile and a wee gurgle. With a happy sigh, I looked at Dot. Nope, no beaming smile on her face, no happy sigh. She was standing, ticket in hand, head looking to the floor. I didn't think we looked like partners, but who knows? Body language is telling, and the way Dot looked at me, smile or no smile, told the blind man on the street that she was my wannabe-partner. I'm pretty sure Stephane got the picture the first day we walked past his window. The bloody dog probably knew too.

Dot kicked her backpack forward, and we shuffled in the queue. I checked her eyes. No tears yet.

'Next!'

Dot moved forward to the check-in desk. I inhaled. This meant I could move forward too, with the rest of my life.

We continued to the next gate, the one where passengers have to take their belts and shoes off, and where ladies need to hand over perfumes and expensive make-up items they forgot to put in their main luggage. Many women have begged to be able to keep their favourite Chanel or Dior perfume but airport staff is trained specifically to deal with these situations. Someone in the training department said the best way to deal with these incidents is to insult the passenger by acting robotically and repeating airport regulations over and over, and never allow the passenger a chance to speak. They are trained to act in groups, circling the passenger. She is, after all, a suspected terrorist, hiding behind the clever guise of carrying Chanel or Dior. If she's lucky she might get the special treatment, where she is ordered to empty all her hand luggage contents onto the stainless steel bench. This is her opportunity to display her spare knickers, her dirty knickers, her tampons, and her pantyliners.

A thick red ribbon forming a maze-like corridor towards the final security gates led to the Passengers Only area. This time I wouldn't be able to pass through.

Dot turned to me with sad eyes. 'Bye,' she said quietly, kissing me on both cheeks.

I grabbed her by her shoulders and looked at her face. No tears. 'Safe flight.' I gave her a hug, thumping her on her back.

She meandered through the ribboned area until she reached the portable doorframe, which she passed through without a beep. There was no stopping and no searching her hand luggage. I smiled her on. She looked back from the other side, once, to give me a quick wave. I waved back. Michael Jackson came into my head. I could hear his girl-boy voice singing, 'She's out of my life'.

As I walked out of the airport, my back straightened, my arms swung freely from side to side, and my eyes shone. I lifted my hands together as if in prayer, and shook them up and down as I processed how well that goodbye went. My head joined in and started nodding up and down. With my nodding head and shaking hands, I walked home, replaying the airport scene. No declarations of love, no pleading gestures, no trembling pouty lips, and no tears. My chest expanded as I breathed deeply.

'It's over,' I said softly to the sky. I pictured my sister, brother, aunts and all my cousins in Australia. 'And my family never found out! Ha ha ha!'

Back on the dangerous balcony, I stretched out on the cushioned chaise longue, glass of wine in one hand, and a slice of pizza from the right in the other. I looked over at the airport and watched the planes line up on the tarmac. Sure enough, I saw an orange and white plane line up. I raised my glass of wine. 'Bon voyage!' I watched that plane like a hawk. I watched it taxi along the tarmac, lift and fly into the air, up and away from me.

Chapter 8

I don't know who was more surprised, Stephane or the dog, as they saw me walking solo, day after day. I wondered if Stephane noted that light spring in my step. Not that he always saw me walk past, cause a lot of the time, I turned right.

I continued my trips to the beach with my green foam mat and my huge homemade cheese and ham baguettes. The beach had changed, however. There was a clear distinction between August 31st and September 1st. On August 31st, it was still very much summer where people wore shorts and t-shirts and went for swims in the sea. The Dream Team were still drinking vodka at 11 a.m. and The Cooler Man was still calling, 'Eeee-eeee-eeee-ooooo-eeee-uuuuuup!' The 1st of September was a different story. Even though the weather was exactly the same as the day before, people suddenly wore trousers and shirts, and fewer people came to the sea for a swim. The kayak dude packed away his kayaks, and the Cooler Man and the Dream Team disappeared. The Desert Rats were still throwing their balls in the sandpit, thank goodness, at least they weren't seasonal. Who knew I would find comfort from the presence of a group of skinny old men?

Dot re-settled into Australia well. She sent updates via email.

'I've bought a new car, moved into a new apartment, and am looking for a new job because my old work hasn't changed a bit. What about you, Baby? Not too lonely?'

I looked around me. The pillows lay in the middle of the sofa bed, my laptop took centre stage on the desk, and in the bathroom, my towel spread across the entire bath rail.

'I'm good, Mate,' I replied, taking a gulp of my wine and shoving a huge piece of blue cheese into my mouth.

I was very happy, but I would have been happier if I didn't get daily emails or texts from Dot. Each morning, as I opened my emails, there she would be.

'Hi Baby! Just wanted to wish you a good day. Enjoy your swim in your gorgeous sea. I'm missing it! x.'

Each evening, my phone vibrated, and there she would be.

"Hi there Mica, what are you doing? Bored yet? Say hi to Stephane for me! x."

For every five times she contacted me, I replied once, always something like, 'Glad you're settling back in. Enjoy that Australian lifestyle, Mate.'

Number One was proud of me. "You've learnt something at least."

She was right, I had learnt. I knew that if I even hinted I was missing her, which I wasn't, or say that I was bored, which I wasn't, that she would be on a long-haul flight into Nice Airport faster than you can say, 'Eeee-eeee-eeee-ooooo-eeee-uuuuuup!'

I didn't have time to get bored between my swimming, my cycling, my writing, and my part-time job. I had found a job teaching English in Sophia Antipolis, a busy little corporate haven. It was a thirty-minute bus ride inland from Nice. I enjoyed the scenery on the way there. In parts, there were mild hills of rocky orange terrain with brushy, harsh trees, reminding me very much of parts of Queensland.

I gave classes to a group of sub-marine engineers at their offices. I tried to maintain a straight face on the first day as I kept recalling the worst chat-up line I'd ever heard from a diver.

In a crowded London bar years before, the diver drunkenly grabbed my face, and slurred, 'Divers go deeper.'

He didn't go anywhere with me.

Fortunately, this group was very well-behaved, and they weren't even divers, they were engineers. They were good learners, a pleasure to teach, and I enjoyed the change in environment. I also enjoyed my end-of-shift treat. Each time class finished, I nipped to the loo to throw on my bikini under my work clothes so that when I got back to Nice, I jumped off the bus, walked to my spot on the beach, stripped off and went swimming. I played, dived, and splashed in the clear aqua sea, until my body was happy to go back to the green mat. I lay in the sun to drip dry, and contentedly listened to the chitter-chatter of French kids. Perfect way to finish a workday.

Soon, it was time to revisit Nice Airport.

'Aaaaaaaaaaaaaaaaaaaaaaaaaaaaaaarrrrrrrrrrrrrrrgh!' I ran towards them. 'So good to see you!' I hugged Cristal and Marilyn tightly, smothering them with Paloma Picasso. 'Did you bring me my Boots order?'

Cristal lifted up her hand luggage. 'Antihistamines, paracetamol, extra-strong mints.'

'Thank you!' I hugged both girls again and led them out of the airport into the sunshine.

'What do you want to see first?' I asked once back at the studio, on the balcony.

Shoving a piece of thin-crust pizza in her mouth, Cristal said, 'The prostitutes!'

'Yes! Later tonight, we'll go for a walk,' I said.

My phone vibrated. Cristal and Marilyn looked at me.

'Is she still texting you daily?' said Marilyn, picking up the wine bottle.

I held my empty glass to her. 'Daily.'

'And emails?' asked Cristal, lifting her glass for a refill too.

'Daily,' I said.

'I don't think it's over,' said Cristal.

'Oh, it's over!' I said, nodding my head more than was necessary.

'Yes,' said Marilyn, taking a sip of her wine, 'it's over. Mica, be clear now. No more leading her on.'

My hand shot up in defence. 'I did not lead her on!'

Cristal and Marilyn reproached me with their looks.

'I didn't!' I said. 'She was somebody you couldn't give an inch to because she took the mile!'

Cristal smacked my head. 'So you don't give the inch,

Stupid!'

'Yeah!' said Marilyn.

The phone vibrated again.

Cristal's eyes softened. 'Ok, she holds on tight.'

'Thank you!'

Cristal held her finger up to me. 'You still played your part!'

Marilyn nodded. 'Yeah!'

I looked up to the sky with resignation. 'I know! Fuck! Fuck! Fuck!' I picked up my glass and proposed a toast. 'Here's to me, not being a selfish shit anymore!'

'Hear, hear!' said Marilyn.

'No more selfish shit!' said Cristal.

'Well? What does the text say?' asked Marilyn, stretching out on her chaise longue.

I picked up my phone. 'Just thinking of you. Missing you. Kiss.'

'And the next text?' asked Cristal.

'PS. I had a croissant today, not half as good as our croissants. Kiss.'

I put the phone down and went back to my pizza.

Cristal walked to the edge of the balcony. 'Who doesn't finish a balcony railing?' she said.

'Maybe he ran out of money?' I lowered my voice to a whisper and pointed. 'He lives downstairs!'

We giggled as we started clearing the plates away.

I boiled the kettle.

Marilyn's eyes shone. 'Hookers?'

'Hookers,' I said, collecting the empty pizza boxes, 'and tomorrow we can visit the Palace in Monaco.'

Cristal laughed. 'Prostitutes and princes! What more could we want?'

September flew by, as did October and November. I was the happiest I had ever been, living in paradise, working, learning French, and ignoring my stalker ex-girlfriend. The texts and emails thankfully had slowed down.

December arrived. It would soon be time for Pere Noël to pay a visit. This meant it was also time for those thoughts to visit. Each December, thoughts of going back to Australia to finish my university degree entered my head.

Number One was an expert at this conversation. She had the speech rehearsed. "We're just going to keep having this conversation each academic year, until you do it. So why not just do it this year? You realise you're not getting younger, don't you?"

Number Two wasn't having it. "Are you crazy? You are finally in a place you love, living a lifestyle you love, and you want to sabotage that, to finish a degree that you are never going to use?"

I nodded my head in agreement.

Number One came back with, "Listen to your gut. Why do we have the same conversation each year? Listen to your gut."

I looked around the studio. The kitchen drawer was full of sparkling new cutlery, including a pizza slicer. The bathroom had a fluffy new bathmat. On the balcony my trusty bikes leant against the half-finished railings, and on the little table lay a new ashtray, a proper one, not made out of foil. I stood sighing as I looked around at my little paradise, and as I did, my hand went to the back of my neck.

I could have punched myself for walking away from that journalism degree years earlier. I started it in Sydney. I had done two years and gotten bored. My friends at the time encouraged me to stay and complete the degree.

'That way, it'll be finished. It'll just be hanging over your head otherwise,' they had said.

I poo-poo'd them. 'No, I don't want to finish it,' I'd said. The problem now of course, was that I did want to finish it, but not because I wanted to be a professional journalist. I wanted to be able to say, "I finished university."

No-one in my family had been to university. My mother had hopes of me becoming a seamstress like Lydia, her sister with the spells. During my highschool years, she paid a seamstress to give me private sewing lessons. The plan was for me to take lessons at the lady's house. I had to walk there after school, via the shops, but the distraction was too much for me. I lost my sewing bag, three times in three weeks.

'Where is it?' said my mother.

'I don't know.' I shrugged.

'Where did you lose it last time?'

'In the Chicky Chicken shop.'

'Well, did you check there?'

'Yes.'

'And?'

'It's not there.'

'Where did you leave it the first time?'

'In Kentucky Fried Chicken.'

'Did you check there?'

'It's not there.'

My mother looked at me like I was deliberately doing this to her.

'I'm not paying for another sewing bag. It's finished!' my mother declared, storming out.

That was the end of my seamstress career, but not the end of my love affair with chicken.

Sitting at my desk in my Nice studio, I scrunched up my face in pain. I closed my eyes and breathed deeply, in and out, for five minutes. The breathing got deeper and louder, until finally I lifted my index finger and slammed it down on the Book Now button on my computer. I hung my head, holding it in my hands, feeling all the blood running out of it. Another five minutes passed before I lifted my heavy head, and stared at the computer screen. My sad eyes were frozen on the screen. The hypnotic tick-tock of the clock hanging on my wall filled the room. I breathed in a final deep breath, pushed my chair away from the desk, stood up and walked away from the computer. Australia here I come.

I didn't like or welcome the change, but everything was changing. Nothing stayed the same. The Dream Team hadn't been there for ages, either had the Cooler Man. The Cooler Man was more than likely getting ready for his winter job, probably as a ski instructor in one of the stations not far from Nice. The dusty Desert Rats were still playing their petanque, that was a comfort at least. The prostitutes were still there too, so it wasn't all bad news.

A long month later, my pilot friend stood at my door, holding my little portable oven.

'Are you sure?' she asked, with a sad smile.

'Yes, take it. I'm just going to have to leave it for my dodgy landlord otherwise.'

'What did he say, when you gave him your notice?'

'Nothing, the lease was renewable or not, after six months.'

'So it was good timing!' she said, a little too enthusiastically.

I watched her boyfriend unchain the bikes from the balcony rail. He wheeled my bike towards the front door.

'I'll be back in a second for the other one,' he said.

When they left, I looked at the balcony, at the empty spot where the bikes used to live, and at the chaises longues which were now cushion-less. I sighed, staring at my view, trying to imprint it, every single detail of it, on my mind.

Two days later, my nose pressed against the plane window. I looked out across the tarmac and up towards the back of Nice, peering to see if I could see my dangerous balcony. I smiled as I realised I could make out the apartment building! I thought I could just about see Stephane's place. My eyes softened when I thought I hadn't even said goodbye to Stephane and his dog, not that I'd visited much in the last months. I hadn't said goodbye to the lady in the high-class bakery either. The last week had been full of doing practical duties, like packing one's life up.

My eyes stayed glued to the plane window, savouring each second, as we started to speed along and upwards. I watched my precious Sud de France home and the chalky aqua water get smaller and smaller. Finally, when I could see nothing but blue, I sank back into my seat and put my hand on my stomach. Chris Isaak's deep voice popped into my head. 'Baby Did A Bad, Bad Thing.' I looked to my right at the guy sitting next to me, half expecting a sympathy look. He didn't look at me. I turned back to the window and studied the plane's wing.

Over an hour later, the voice said, 'Ladies and Gentlemen, welcome to London where the temperature is a pleasant twelve degrees and the time is twelve-forty five. Thank you for flying with us and we wish you a pleasant stay.'

Shortly after, I walked out of the baggage claim area with my backpack. I popped into Boots for a soothing squirt of

Estee Lauder's Must, before buying a ticket for the Gatwick Express.

At Victoria, I passed my Costa Coffee kiosk, but no time for coffee, I continued through the uninterested, non-eye-contact-making masses, to get the crowded tube up to Finchley Park, where I changed and got on the double-decker, to my final destination.

My mood lifted once I stepped into leafy Crouch End. The excitement of seeing my friends had put a smile on my face. The smile grew wider as I climbed the hill opposite the park I knew so well, to reach Marilyn's flat.

'Hello?' said Marilyn's voice through her intercom.

'It's me, open the bloody door.'

'Hoorah! Come up!'

Marilyn buzzed me in, and my feet automatically took me up the narrow staircase to the top floor, where Marilyn stood, with a bottle of wine in her hand.

Marilyn, her sister Malina, and I did what we always did whenever I came around to their flat. We ate a curry around Marilyn's chunky wooden kitchen table, and we drank, smoked, and played DJ with Marilyn's excellent music collection.

The table was strewn with bottles, corks, plates of half-finished curry, bowls with dips and poppadoms, and ashtrays full of butts.

'Make space, make space,' slurred Marilyn.

She was the shortest of us, and the wine always got to her

first.

Malina and I took the empty bottles off the table and lined up them against the wall, on the floor.

'Who's responsible for this debauchery?' Malina moved from bottle to bottle. 'Is it you Pinot Grigio? No? Is it you Chardonnay? No? Sauvignon Blanc? Who's responsible?'

Kenny Roger's voice came through the speakers and we ran to stand in line. Marilyn positioned herself between Malina and me. We sang, 'Lucille,' to the fridge in our loudest voices.

As the song progressed, Malina and I got louder, and Marilyn got creative with her dance moves. The neighbours must have been overjoyed.

An hour later, just as Neil Diamond sang, 'I am, I said,' Marilyn said, 'Let's go to the pub.'

At the pub, I made a whole new group of friends within half an hour. This has happened before.

I visited my friend Shelly in Pisa a few years back. She had been living there for four years. I went for four days and by day two, I had my very own set of friends. It happened organically, or perhaps better said, alcoholically. Shelly told me on Day One that she would take me to a bar in the centre.

'We must have aperitivi,' she said. 'We'll go for happy hour.'

We walked over cobbled streets, past the gelato place that, once they saw how many times I visited in one day, gave me a 'get the tenth free' card, to a small colourful bar.

We were greeted with a warm smile from the barmaid.

'Spritz per favore, due,' said Shelly taking a seat at the bar and flashing the waitress her crazy beautiful smile.

I took the stool next to her. I looked around at the friendly room filled with small groups of lively people, sitting at tables with lots of colourful drinks.

Shelly said, 'Let's get some aperitivis.'

At the buffet table, Shelly's face lit up when she saw the mini proscuitto pastries. I took a plate and filled it with olives, cheese, and salsa chips.

Back at the bar, we lifted our Spritz's. 'Cheers!'

I raised my glass, delighted to have, not only my sense of sight being overloaded, but my hearing too. Laughter filled the bar, and the warm and animated sound of Italian being spoken, almost drowned out the funky bar music.

Shelly's friends, all English Teachers, tumbled into the bar half an hour later.

'Hello,' said a man in beige trousers and a white business shirt, taking my hand. 'I'm Andy.'

Andy had a southern accent.

'Hello. Mica,' I said, smiling, shaking his hand.

'Michelle.' Michelle was next to shake my hand.

She was a very thin woman with very thin brown hair. Michelle had something northern about her accent. She was going to have to talk more, so I could confirm that.

'Hi, I'm Lizzie,' said a young black woman, wearing a multi-coloured dress and boots. 'Nice to meet you,' she said, shaking my hand.

Lizzie had a London accent.

The last one to introduce himself was huffing David.

'Hi there,' huffed an overweight and very smiley man, 'I see you got here! Shelly was wondering if you'd have any travel difficulties, but obviously not. Well done.' He smiled. Before I could say anything, he slapped his forehead. 'Oh bloody hell, sorry!' He stretched out his hand, 'I'm David.'

David was maybe Cambridge or Oxford, and utterly delightful.

'Oh flippin' heck,' said Michelle, pulling up a stool, 'I really do need a drink, what after the day I've had and all.'

I took a sip of my Spritz, silently confirming Michelle was northern.

Shelly beamed her lovely smile towards the waitress. 'Sie Spritz per favore!'

The night turned into dinner across the road where we had the freshest and tastiest pizza I'd ever had, no disrespect to my South of France colleagues. Dinner was followed by a bar above the restaurant, lots of scotch and cokes, and lots of random conversations with very nice-smelling Italian guys, followed by being swept away by one of them, a certain crazy curly-haired Giovanni. We met his cool friends in another bar, and consequently, three days of Giovanni romance and mayhem followed.

'Thanks for having me!' I said, giving Shelly a kiss at the train station on my last day. 'I had a fab time!' I shoved my gelati card into her hand, there was only one more stamp to go.

'I know you did,' said Shelly, 'but it wasn't with me. I hardly saw you!'

'Ma, che cosa dice?' I teased her, picking up my bag.

'Four days and she speaks the language, and she's got her own friends. Brava! Get on the bloody train!' Shelly planted a big fat wet kiss on my cheek and pushed me on board.

'Arrivederci, Bella!' I shouted, blowing her one last happy kiss.

The pub in Crouch End was loud. My new group of friends included a tall guy with long blond dreadlocks. I had clocked him the minute I walked into the pub, and without a word of warning to the girls, I walked over to stand near the group. Marilyn and Malina watched me from the front door of the pub.

'She's going for the guy with the dreads,' they slurred, totally au fait with my desertion.

'Hi,' said tall Mr Dreads, smiling down at me.

'I like your dreads,' I said.

'Thanks, I like your tan. You look healthy.'

'I'm not.'

Mr Dreads laughed and took me to the bar to buy me a

drink. I liked the feel of his strong arm guiding me. While he ordered drinks, I took the chance to look at him properly. He was tall, and had a thin but strong-looking body. He wore green jeans and a white t-shirt.

'Here you are,' he said, handing me a glass of white wine. 'Cheers!'

He had an open, friendly face. I found myself relaxing even more than I already was.

'To a fun night,' said Mr Dreads, lifting his glass to his lips. A little twinkle appeared in his blues eyes, and I happily mirrored the action with my brown eyes.

The next day, still drunk, reeking of fags and booze, dressed in last night's clothes, I pressed Marilyn's buzzer.

'Eh?' Marilyn's hungover voice came through the intercom.

'Eh,' my hungover voice replied.

The door buzzed, and I crawled up the eternal narrow staircase. Marilyn slumped by the door in her white dressing robe. Her blonde bed hair hung across her hungover face.

'You have one night in London and you manage to pick up,' she said.

I stumbled into the flat. 'He had dreads.'

'You should be anti-dreadlocked. Want a drink?'

'No. I've got to get to the airport. Shower first.'

That was my London stop-over. In fact, that was my

London life beforehand; always boozing, smoking, and eating with Marilyn and friends. I loved every toxic minute back in the day.

I felt justified sleeping with Mr Dreads. I liked the feel of his rough skin. My body had responded well. Of course, it had happened while I was plastered, a familiar old pattern. Not to be too negative, I realised I had figured out a few things about men, and one thing I knew for sure, is that not all men are rapists, in fact, some are very much the gentleman. A little piece of toffee must have fallen off me.

On the train to Heathrow, my mind wasn't worried about gender, it was back to familiar conversations.

Number One said, "You're shameless. How can you sleep with someone you don't even know? You put yourself in danger. You could have been killed. How can you?"

Number Two was still in impressed mode. "Oh my God, you're so much fun!"

The Personality Twins went back and forwards with each other. I let them fight it out.

"Irresponsible!"

"Fun!"

"Irresponsible!"

"Fun!"

The train moved away from London and towards Heathrow, travelling past rows of joined-together brown houses.

In the airport, I meandered through the ribboned maze and through the portable security doorframe to collect my hand luggage.

'Excuse me, Ma'am? Is this your bag?' I was stopped by an airport worker.

I sighed.

'Can you please open it and empty the contents?' said the expressionless Airport Worker.

I sighed, again. Opening my bag, my hands went straight to it. 'Here,' I held up my half-used Estee Lauder perfume. 'Would you like my foundation too?'

'I'm just following airport regulations, Ma'am,' said Mr Zero Personality Airport Worker, taking the perfume and foundation.

As I put my knickers, tampons, and panty liners back in my handbag, Number One said, "And you knew, but because you were so hungover, you forgot. Who's fun now?"

I consoled myself later in the perfume part of Duty Free by spraying on half the shop. Then, I went across to Boots for more of the same. I love Boots. When people ask me what I like about living in the UK, I say, 'Boots.' After walking around the shop in circles, I finally bought paracetamol. I bought Ibuprofen too. I bought a can of Orange Fanta too.

In the waiting hall, I took two paracetamol tablets with my Fanta. Finishing the can in two gulps, I walked to the rubbish bin and passed by a well-dressed man on my right.

He looked at me. We made eye contact for less than a second, but in that millisecond I had clocked his body, his hair, his eyes, and the one-second meaningful look he had given me.

My body had followed through, sending out a sign saying, "Yes, I see you see me. I see you too. Yes, I would."

I smiled. I thought back to the lovely rough skin of Mr Blond Dreads, and to this handsome man just now. My body was acting independently of the brain, and certainly of Personality Number One. My body was reacting naturally. I stopped walking and gasped as I made the realisation. My body was definitely noticing men! A smile broke out on my tired, hungover face. Could it be I was finally, finally, finally ready for a relationship with a man?

'Flight number X9927 is ready for boarding. Please proceed to Gate 15,' the voice said.

Taking a deep alcohol-saturated breath, I walked towards the boarding gate, with a lazy, man-loving smile on my face. Yes Sir, I can boogie.

Chapter 9

'Excuse me, Ma'am? We'll be landing soon. Could you please close your tray?'

Meanwhile, another flight attendant walked up and down the aisles spraying us with God knows what, for quarantine purposes.

We landed shortly after and soon I was walking through Sydney customs, passing numerous smiling airport employees. What a difference to Heathrow.

I walked out of the airport and into brilliant sunlight, blinking at the brightness. The colours were on high definition. The sky was super blue, the trees were super green, and the birds were super shiny. The place looked like it had been washed with BriteLite. I looked up to check Doris Day wasn't about to come dancing out of the clouds.

I stayed with my friend, Casey, in Manly. Casey is a dentist and has a spacious two-bedroom flat with water views.

'Your room,' she pointed to a blue room.

'Thanks.' I dumped my bags and went to join her in the lounge. Blue water glistened in the distance. 'Nice view.'

'Yes,' she said, handing me a glass of champagne. 'Cheers! To you, coming back to finish your degree!'

'Cheers! And thank you again,' I said, 'it's just till I find a place.'

'No rush,' said Casey. 'It's nice to have you back after so

many years.'

'Don't get used to it,' I said, 'once the year is finished, I'm going straight back.'

'We'll see,' she said.

I looked at her glowing face. Casey is the type of woman who gets more beautiful with age. She has enormous blue eyes, full lips, and shoulder-length blonde hair which sits around her pretty face. I said, 'You look good! You look great actually!'

'Thanks.'

She could have said, "You too," but she didn't cause we are true friends, and I had just spent far too long on a plane, whilst hungover.

The next day, Casey had to leave for work at eight.

'Remember where everything is?' she said, standing at the front door.

'Yep.'

When I studied the first part of my degree, I had lived not too far away.

'Got your keys?' Casey said.

'I'm good. Go, go. I'll text you if I get lost,' I joked.

She closed the door, and I sank down on the sofa in her sun-filled living room, with my coffee.

My phone vibrated. Mango answered my text from last night. "Glad you got in well! Welcome Home! Maybe you'll find an Aussie fella? x"

I smiled at Mango's priorities. Maybe she was right, who knew?

Mid-morning, freshly-showered and feeling slightly more normal, I stepped out of the flat into the bright sunshine, to take the ten-minute walk to Manly centre. I walked past modern houses with long verandahs and spacious front lawns, till I got to the water and followed the path towards the centre. The blue water glistened under the morning sun and little rowing boats bobbed up and down in the calm waters. Along the shore, a bronzed man, and a woman wearing a sports bikini, carried their kayaks.

The scenery was calming. I strolled along, deliberately taking my time to enjoy the new sights and sounds. The water lapped on the shore, a boat started its motor, and further along, water slushed as a big ferry came in, slowing to a stop at the dock. In the park, dogs barked, birds chirped and cars whizzed alongside not too far away. Children played in a little sandpit. They had little Australian voices.

'Did you see me, Mum?'

Parents had big Australian voices.

'Yeah, I saw you, Robbie. Very good.'

The parents sat on nearby benches, drinking takeaway coffee and watching their kids through sunglasses.

I looked around me.

"This is nice," said Number One.

"This is pleasant," said Number Two. "Not quite the Promenade Des Anglais, is it?"

"Give it a chance," said Number One.

I continued walking across the road to the shopping area. A sporty couple, in swimmers, carried their surfboards across the pedestrian-only street towards the surf beach. They moved fast, so as not to burn their bare feet on the clay pavement. I took a seat on a bench. My tooshie got a shock. It was only mid-morning, but already the bench was hot from the sun. With my sunglasses on, I people-watched as bodies walked to get to the calm beach, or in the other direction, the surf beach.

All body types walked past. There were fit bodies and not-so-fit bodies. Without realising, I stared at one of these not-so-fit fellows. My eyes travelled from his scruffy hair and his lazy smile, down to his singlet which clung over a proper round beer belly. My eyes did a u-turn and went back to look at his chubby arms, the tops of which had little hairs growing on them. Then my eyes went to his short shorts, his stubby legs, and finally to his feet, on which he wore his well-worn rubber thongs.

Mr Scruffy saw me staring. 'Why don't ya take a picture?' he said, in his Australian drawl.

'Excuse me,' I said, unable to break my stare.

'What's wrong with ya? Take a bloody picture!' he mocked as he walked away.

I felt my chest and face burn in shame, but my eyes had already fixed on two chubby teenage girls walking towards the surf side. They wore tight tops and their chubby stomachs pushed out over their hipster shorts, giving them the muffin-top look. Overtaking them was a fit young man, wearing red shorts, a magnificent tan, and a huge smile. On this day, there seemed to be no in between. The common factor was they all wore genuine smiles.

Years earlier, I had taught English to adult foreigners in Manly. I'd asked the class to read a newspaper article each and present it to the class.

My dainty Japanese student, her name was Akiko but she asked us to call her Athena, as in Warrior Princess, got up and said, 'This news article talks about foods. Fast foods. This article says that fast foods makes you happy. I think this must be true because Australia people are very, very happy.'

I nodded at her logic, and so did the students. We all got it. The insult was delivered so beautifully. We applauded. Top marks! The Vietnamese student then stood up and said that in Vietnam, people ate more healthily. When asked to give an example, he talked about vegetables and seafood. He proceeded to delight his fellow students and me, by giving an animated masterclass on the best way to catch an eel in the mud.

It had been many years since I had been in Manly. Everything was familiar, yet different. Despite the beauty, the spaciousness, and the friendliness, I felt enormous separation anxiety from France. I immediately started doing the inevitable and comparing everything. As I walked past the bakery, I looked down at the plastic-looking, oversized pastries in the window, sitting on plastic trays. There were no handmade baskets, ribbons, or cellophane. The smell didn't smell of nurture or buttery divinity. Next door, the butcher had no livers or kidneys in the window, no pigs' feet, and no skinned rabbits. People didn't say hello when they walked into a shop either, they just walked in.

"It's not like that in France." The thought popped into my head and I gasped, putting my hand over my open mouth. I had become a Maria-Louisa. Oh my Gawd!

It didn't stop with the bakery or the butcher. Walking out of the bank, I gasped when the bank teller said, 'Have a good day, Sweetheart.'

Not long after the bank, I was accosted by a wildlife charity fundraiser. He was a tall guy dressed in a smelly, old, matted Koala suit. The giant Koala danced on the spot, waving and shaking his money bucket.

'No thanks,' I said, walking past, the guilt already starting to seep in.

The Koala spoke back, in a cheerful voice. 'No worries, Buddy!'

I started to understand I needed to readjust to the friendly Australian familiarity. "Madame" was long gone. I hung my head and mourned, walking along the pedestrian street.

Things got worse when I walked into Coles supermarket, one of the bigger supermarket chains. I stood at the cheese section looking from left to right, and my face became paler by the second. My eyes searched for more cheese, for fresh cheese, not plastic-covered blocks of cheese. I turned in circles, looking behind me. Surely there must be more cheese than this? Where was the goddamn cheese? I started to hyperventilate.

"Where is the real cheese!?" I screamed inside.

Alas, there was no real cheese in this supermarket. There was bread, though. Lots of it. It was white, sliced, and in plastic bags.

"It's not like this in France," I said in my head, visualising Maria-Louisa and cringing at myself.

The shock didn't stop there.

'Let's have dinner together tonight,' Casey had said before she left the flat that morning.

My job was to get us a bottle of wine. I went to the bottle shop.

Back at Casey's apartment, I placed the wine bottle on the kitchen bench with a bang. 'I had to pay six dollars for this bottle of wine!'

Casey stopped cutting the spring onions and stared at me. 'Six dollars?'

'Yes!' I shook my head and shrugged my shoulders. 'I couldn't find the other wine. I tried. I looked all over the shop. This was actually the cheapest they had. It had better be good.'

Casey laughed, and continued to laugh. She laughed while she finished cutting the spring onions, she laughed while she added the snow peas to the wok, and she laughed when she stirred the chicken pieces in.

The wine was dreadful, and we both suffered very bad hangovers the next day.

'No more cheap wine, Mica,' said Casey, swallowing a paracetamol tablet.

'Yes, I understand,' I said, lying on the sofa, holding my throbbing head.

The minimum price for a decent bottle of wine in Australia was ten dollars, according to Casey, the very minimum. I hadn't realised just how accustomed I had been to paying three euros for a bottle in France. Ten dollars seemed absurd. This was about to pose a grave problem for me, in my impoverished student state. I was in a tricky situation because I needed to drink, to deal with the culture shock.

Within a month, I found myself a little studio in an inner-city suburb called Mosman. Mosman is a mix of beautifully maintained older houses plus some designer modern ones, and some apartment blocks. The suburb is upmarket. Not as much white sliced bread in Mosman, just lots of baguettes, focaccias, ciabattas, sourdough loaves, mixed grain loaves, linseed loaves, and you-name-it loaves. There was cheese too, real cheese, and coffee shops selling fifty types of coffee. Mosman is "Ooorstraarliyah" style in its culture and it is also very pretty to look at. You walk up and down hilly tree-lined streets with lots of greenery and birdlife, until you hit the sparkling champagne waters of Sydney Harbour.

At the bottom of my leafy street was the ferry dock. I planned to take the ferry to university each day.

On my first day, the ferryman, dressed in navy shorts and work boots, gave me a big smile as I walked up the plank. 'Morning!' His smile was as wide as the harbour.

'Morning!'

I went up to the upper deck, took a seat and looked around at the empty seats.

"Where the fuck is everyone?" Number Two asked.

In London, I caught the tube, and even in Nice, the buses were crowded, but here, it looked as if the business couple on the lower deck, plus myself, had chipped in and chartered the ferry to take us to the Opera House. Our ferry putt-putted off, and even though the waters were clear of other boat traffic, we cruised at a snail's pace, making a few stops at the nearby water-front neighbourhoods along the way. With each agonising slow pull in and slow pull out of the ferry stops, I tapped my fingers and rolled my eyes.

The best way I'd ever travelled to a job before was by skiing. I was the receptionist of a hotel in Meribel, a French but very British ski resort. I had to be at work for seven in the morning to set up the breakfast room. I lived up the mountain, and the buses didn't run early.

'Non Madame, desole, le bus ne commence pas avant sept heure et demi,' the man at the tourist office had said.

So, each morning, I woke up, put on my work uniform, then over that, my ski jacket, pants, gloves, and boots. I walked the one hundred metres over crunchy morning snow to the solitary piste and in total silence and near-darkness, snowploughed down to work.

Pulling into Circular Quay dock on my first day, a huge smile came across my face as I saw the iconic Opera House. She sat beautifully on the point, welcoming visitors of every nationality. I jumped off the ferry and walked through the central business district streets, past rushing businessmen and women, towards Hyde Park. Ten minutes later, I stood before the brown-stoned building which would be my place of study for the next year.

When I had told Marilyn and Cristal about returning to university to complete the degree, they had both had the same reaction, 'Why?!'

'So that it is done, and I can move forward. Otherwise each year I'll think about it.'

'But you're so happy in your life now!'

'I know, I know. I will come straight back to it. And, it might be interesting going back to uni, using my brain again, you know?'

I had visions of books, broadening my perspectives and being mentally stimulated. The degree I was finishing was a Bachelor of Arts, and although one might argue it might not be the most intellectually stimulating, I had hoped it would be at least challenging.

It wasn't. We had one principal tutor who was about three years older than me. He had never, ever, worked outside of an academic environment. I nicknamed him Mr Aussie Ocker. Mr Aussie Ocker was tall, with an average build. He had short dark hair but at the front it was long, and it flopped over his left eye when lecturing, or as I would come to understand, regurgitating information. His accent was his most distinct feature. It was strong and conjured up images of outback Australia. If I closed my eyes while he talked, I could see wild horses galloping, crocodiles thrashing in swamps, and kangaroos bouncing across flat fields. Each time he said, 'Good morning,' I could touch orange dust, flick flies from my hot face, and feel the sweat trickle down my back.

Mr Aussie Ocker lectured on creating a present from historical past actions, and being responsible for the present. Ironically, the present for him, a few months into the course, was an unruly class of privileged twenty-year-olds. Mr Aussie Ocker had established zero authority from the beginning, because his classroom management skills consisted of bargaining, pleading, and threatening.

'Oh, come on you guys. You guys! Come on. Settle down, you guys.'

His whiny Australian accent got to me every fucking time.

'No, it's not fair to the people who want to be here.' Mr Aussie Ocker shrugged his cardigan-wearing shoulders, and his eyes pleaded with the loud twenty-year-olds to behave. He sighed, and walked up and down, shaking his head. The twenty-year-olds continued talking and laughing, getting louder by the second. 'No, come on, you guys. If you continue,' one hand would go on his hip, the other hand in the air, finger pointing, 'if you continue, I'm gonna... I'm gonna... I'm gonna... well, I don't know what I'm gonna do! There! Are you happy?'

I wasn't happy. I wasn't happy at all. Aware of my extravagant student fees, I couldn't believe that I was paying for this circus day in, day out. I was in Aussie Ocker hell and I wanted him to admit he had created his present and take responsibility. Ironically, I also was responsible for my current reality. At least I was accompanied by two other mature-age students. They were just as pissed off as me and they had words with Mr Aussie Ocker who said he would handle it, but who continued to fail spectacularly throughout the entire year.

The unruly twenty-year-olds, if undisciplined, were an extremely sweet bunch at heart. It had been a long time since I'd been twenty and I had forgotten what the important things were at that age.

'Oh my God! I love your sunglasses,' said the twenty-year-old to my left.

The twenty-year-old to my right, said, 'Oh my God! I love your handwriting!'

I smiled. It was excruciating, yet delightful.

My two new university twenty-year-old friends were complete opposites. One was a virgin who had a very strict Egyptian father.

'I've never been drunk. What's it like?' said the young maiden. Her large brown eyes were covered with a million gorgeous thick eye-lashes. She stared at me, blinking slowly and waiting for an answer.

The other was a scrawny bottle-blonde who wore short skirts, high heels, and far too much make-up. 'My mum loves it when my boyfriend stays over.'

Blondie turned out to be a Straight-A student. She knew exactly how and what to re-regurgitate to impress Mr Aussie Ocker. She consistently scored better than me, much better.

Every spare second I wasn't studying, I was working. I had to pay the Mosman rent and be able to eat and drink, but not as often as I'd like, due to the unexpected inflation in the price of wine. I got a job working in a maternity boutique up the road from my studio in beautiful "Ooorstraarliyah" Mosman.

A week after I started, Charlotte, my manager, said, 'You know what's funny? I had a dream last night that you were a lesbian.'

I raised my eyebrows. 'Oh?'

Number One laughed. "I had a nightmare that you were a lesbian, for much longer than you should have been."

'Are you going to Mardi Gras?' asked Charlotte.

My face brightened with the thought. 'I love the drag queens!'

'Me too! Where are you going to be for the parade?'

Moira and Elisa, my very dear friends, had been around at my place for dinner the week earlier. It had been so heartwarming to see them again after so long.

'We hear you had a lady relationship,' teased Moira, my lesbian friend, over dinner. Her brown eyes sparkled, lighting up her delicate face.

'And I will never have another,' I said, lifting my glass of wine.

Her partner, Elisa, joined in. 'When are you going to come out, Mica?'

'Nothing to come out to, my friend.'

'Sure?' Elisa's green eyes bore into mine. Her look was

questioning and sultry.

I met her provoking look and held it. I had always been attracted to Elisa. She was witty and had a dry sense of humour. I admired her. She was a strong woman with a good job that she loved. I liked her sense of self, and for some confusing reason, I always found I wanted to flirt with her. I wanted to tease her and make her laugh. I did not, however, want to know anything about her breasts or vagina.

'Sure,' I replied to Elisa's tease.

Moira and Elisa, the power couple, had a magnificent terrace home in inner-city Paddington, on Oxford Street, where the Sydney Mardi Gras Parade would pass along. They kindly provided their large balcony for our little group of friends to watch the razzle-dazzle. They provided the food too. The gourmet buffet, beautifully presented on the balcony table, had nothing from a supermarket in it. This was Moira's and Elisa's house, after all. You only get the good stuff. Even the dog gets organic food. I know this because years earlier they had brought the dog around to mine for the weekend, for me to dogsit while they flew to a spa weekend.

When they came back to get him, Moira asked, 'Was he good?'

'He was lovely, good company. He shared my Coco Pops.'

Moira clutched at her bony chest. 'You gave him Coco Pops?' She pulled the dog towards her.

'He loves them,' I said, baffled.

As Elisa shoved the dog and one distressed Moira into the car that day, she whispered in my ear, 'She only gives him pigs' ears, specially bought from a farm.'

The same dog was now happily playing amongst us on the modern Paddington balcony.

'Try the smoked salmon,' Elisa passed me a glass, and pointed to the silver platter on the table.

'Thanks,' I said, my greedy eyes scanning the buffet. I noted the big fat black olives, the Parma ham wrapped around anchovies, and the freshly sliced mango.

The dog was eyeing up the good stuff too. I looked at him. His eyes were clear, his fur was shiny, and his nose was wet. He was the epitome of health, no doubt due to his organic diet.

Elisa came back to me, holding a champagne bottle. She gestured for my glass.

'Dykes On Bikes will be coming through soon,' she said, topping up my champagne. 'Sure you don't want to join them, Mica?'

My eyes smiled. 'Stop fantasizing, Elisa. You'd like to see me dressed in leather. I know. I see how you look at me.'

Elisa threw her head back and laughed.

Moira looked over. 'What's so funny?'

'Nothing,' we replied in unison.

I joined Casey, we leaned on the balcony to look down to the street. I looked at the solid steel balcony railings. My eyes followed them round to the very end.

Number Two was ahead of me. "These are proper railings."

'Thank God we're up here,' Casey said.

I looked down at the people squashed together on the street below. 'I know. Look at it. It's jam-packed.'

A horn sounded from the street.

'It's starting!' yelled Moira.

Our friends left the beautiful buffet food to come and stand next to Casey and me, leaning on the lovely, strong, polished, professional rails.

At street level, the first float started moving forward. A group of half-naked men, dressed as angels, danced, their silver wings flapping in time to the music. I danced too, swinging my hips to 'We are family'.

Following the silver angels came a parade of tinsel, sparkles, stilettos, wigs, extravagant make-up, body oil, boots, bronzer, feathers, more bronzer, ego, and a whole load of *glam, bam, thank you ma'am*.

From the comfort of the balcony, we cheered on the floats whilst sipping champagne. 'Bravo!' we cheered. 'Whoop, whoop, whoop!'

The ambiance on the street was fabulous, and so was the ambiance on our balcony.

'There she is.' Casey pointed down to an older woman, marching amongst forty young men wearing teeny tiny pink shorts and pink boots. The woman was dressed in comfortable flat shoes, pastel blue linen trousers, and an oversized t-shirt. 'Mum's come out to support her gay son.'

I watched her walking in the midst of the pink, waving her little rainbow flag.

'Yep, probably left her husband at home,' I said. 'She probably said, "He's my son too, Kevin, and I love him and I support him and his partner. I'm going to the parade. You just watch me."'

Casey laughed at my super strong mock Australian accent. 'And here she is, bless her pastel cotton socks,' Casey said, pointing.

'Bravo, Mum!' We cheered Mum on from above, raising our glasses to her.

We heard motorbike revs getting closer.

'Dykes on bikes!' squealed Casey. 'They're coming!'

I leant back and glanced past Casey, to Elisa at the other end of the balcony, to see her looking over at me. She winked, and I laughed.

Our balcony party guzzled champagne and enjoyed the parade till the very end.

'Good job, boys!' We cheered the last little float passing by. It was a tractor, decorated in the colours of the rainbow, driven by two magnificent bronzed men in silver overalls.

Honk! Honk! They beeped their horn and waved at the crowds.

People in the street followed behind the tractor, effectively signalling the end of the parade, and closing the road, to create a massive street party.

'Thanks, Moira,' I kissed her on both cheeks, holding my handbag. 'Thank you for everything. It was a brilliant night, and the food was divine!'

'You're welcome!' Moira tilted her head, exposing her elegant neck.

'Elisa,' I walked over to her. 'Thank you! As always, a pleasure!'

She looked at me with twinkling eyes. 'You are going to join the parade next year, aren't you?'

'Yes, if my family find out about Dot, they'll have me on a float decorated with a Virgin Mary and a wooden stake,' I said.

Elisa laughed. 'Yes, and you'll be carried along by men dressed as altar boys.'

'Yes, they will be praying for me the whole length of the parade. And let's not forget the mariachi band following behind.'

Elisa laughed again. 'Seriously though, you enjoyed yourself tonight. Admit it,' she said.

'Yes.'

'So, Australia is not that bad, after all?'

'It is too!' I snapped in a fake huff.

'No, it isn't.'

'Yes, it is.'

Elisa's green eyes looked into mine. 'Did you enjoy yourself tonight?'

'Very much.'

'So no, it isn't,' said Elisa, practically pushing me out the door.

I looked around for Casey. 'Ready?'

Casey said her goodbyes, and we walked down the stairs. Elisa stood at the door, waving bye.

I yelled up, 'You always have to have the last word.'

'No, I don't!' she said, quickly slamming the door.

Down on street level, Casey and I made our way through heaving, sweaty, half-naked, dancing people, blowing whistles and horns. We walked towards the ferry dock at Circular Quay.

Twenty minutes later, the contrast in environment was enormous. Casey and I sailed to our respective homes, her to Manly, me to Mosman, under the moonlight, listening to the sound of gentle waves.

Two days later in the maternity boutique, I compared Mardi Gras notes with Charlotte, my manager.

'I think some of them must be qualified make-up artists,' I said, placing a two hundred dollar teddy bear in the display window. Charlotte folded designer maternity jeans. 'I know! It must take them hours to get ready. And how do they walk in those stilettos?'

I liked working in the maternity boutique. It brought out the nurturer in me. I enjoyed helping the women and their partners. The couples were in such a state of bliss, that they couldn't help but wish the same joy for everyone, including for me.

Each shift, whilst handing the customer their change, they asked, 'And you?'

'Hmmm?' I said, pretending I didn't know what was coming.

'How many children do you have?'

'Oh, I don't have any children,' I said, waiting for the reaction.

Three seconds later, there it was. The woman had a fallen face. Two seconds later, so did the husband.

'Oh.' A little encouraging smile came forth from the woman. 'It's not too late, but even still, tick tock, tick tock.'

The same conversation happened so often that for the first time in my life, I began to question my barren status. What was wrong with me? No children? What on earth had I been thinking? The pity on the customers' faces got so much that I began dreading going into work because I couldn't bear to disappoint everyone.

I came up with a brilliant solution.

'And you?' a woman asked, handing over money whilst I wrapped her stretchy jeans.

'Hmmm?'

'How many children do you have?' she said, patting her six-month stomach.

'Still trying!' I shot her my most hopeful smile.

Her face brightened, and she stretched her hand out to me. 'It took us ages, so keep trying, you'll get there!'

'Yes.' I smiled in return.

The new strategy was genius, truly genius, until it backfired. We had a lot of repeat customers because as a woman grew in size, she obviously needed more clothes. There was one particular gorgeous couple who were a delight to serve because they brimmed with joy. However, because I was obliged to maintain my "Still trying!" facade throughout her entire pregnancy, we got to the stage where they walked into the shop, the husband looked to me expectantly, I shook my head, and he would slump his shoulders. So in effect, they walked in happy and expectant, but walked out disappointed. My strategy was back-firing and the energy it took to constantly lie was leaving me exhausted.

Life, in general, was exhausting me. I was living in a country I didn't want to live in, studying in a circus, and pretending to be trying get pregnant with a pretend partner. It seemed if I wasn't pretending at one thing, I was pretending at another. Would I ever grow up and be a real adult? Would I ever have a normal relationship, and if so, when?

Chapter 10

My university year in Mosman was not my most balanced. All I did was study and work.

'Want to go to that Mexican restaurant Moira was talking about?' Casey asked.

'Can't afford it.'

'Want to see a movie this week?'

'Can't afford it.'

'Want to go to the zoo? I've got discounted tickets.'

'Still can't afford it.'

'What can you afford?'

'Nothing.'

Casey smiled. 'What about a walk? Around The Spit?'

'Yes!' I said. 'Walking is recommended for pregnant women.'

'Still playing that game?'

'It's hard to give up once you've started. They keep fucking coming back for more clothes.'

People in Europe had often asked me why I left Australia. Walking around The Spit area, looking at the spacious houses, the wide streets, the pretty parks, the spectacular harbour, and the blue skies, I could understand why they asked. Sydney couldn't be more beautiful if it tried. In certain areas, of course. The answer as to why I left? I just always knew it wasn't for me. Whilst I appreciate all the positives about my country, I have a thing for Europe. It's like falling in love. Sometimes you can't pinpoint what it is about that person, you just know that you love them. I love Europe, simple as that. One might say it's because it's the opposite of Australia, but in fact, in my experience, I found certain aspects of life in the south of France to be similar to Australia. I found some of the men to be similar; muscular and straight-talking. No disrespect to the UK, but if I caught a taxi in the UK, the male taxi driver is not necessarily going to help me with my heavy baggage (generally speaking, I know, I know, I know the argument). In Australia or the south of France, the male taxi driver isn't going to bother with the pleasantries, he's just going to pick up your heavy suitcase and throw it in the car. Generally speaking again.

On a train pulling into Clapham Station one wintery London day, everyone moved forward to the doors, squashing together. The train hadn't even stopped yet and people were adjusting their coats and arranging their bags in preparation for the doors opening. A young mother, with a toddler and a baby in a stroller, was by the doors. When the doors opened, she lifted the baby in the stroller down first, leaving the toddler to wait. The people on the train walked around the waiting toddler and got off. No-one offered to help, myself included. The little toddler stood waiting, but before his mother could get back to him, an Australian guy whisked the kid into the air and planted him firmly down on the platform.

'There you go, little man,' he said in his broad accent, before walking off.

I'm not saying he was right, and I'm not saying he was

wrong, and I'm not saying that any other nationality person would or wouldn't have done the same. I'm just saying I think he must have been new into the country.

Having said all this, I still prefer to live in the UK over Australia because although I love sports, I am more culture over sports. Also, half of my family live in the UK. My father's family is from Liverpool. In the early sixties, my father left Liverpool and went to work as a dive engineer, building a bridge in Acajutla in El Salvador. That's how he met my mother. A group of Brits, Germans, and Americans was there to build the bridge. My mother and her friends were the domestic help. They wore white aprons over long grey dresses, tights, and lace-up shoes. They also wore white cotton headbands to cover their hair, which was pulled back in tight buns. The women were immaculate, not a thread out of place.

The girls held open the kitchen door just enough to peer into the next room, where the foreign men sat around a big table.

'Who's going to serve them coffee?'

'I don't speak English!' said a Salvadoreña, pressing down her starched uniform with anxious hands.

'Me neither,' said another, smoothing her neat bun.

My mother picked up the coffee tray and walked into the next room.

White men, puffing thick cigars, looked up.

With her back straight, my mother said in a clear voice, 'Quien va querer cafe?'

The men sitting around the table, under a slow-turning ceiling fan, looked at her.

My father raised his hand, and said, 'Lo tomo sin leche y con dos de azucar.'

I could never figure out how my parents got together. My father was calm, responsible, and quiet. My mother was loud, demanding, and fiery. I couldn't see it. Then when I was twenty-one, I went to Liverpool for the first time and met the women in my Liverpudlian family. Then I saw it.

Walking around The Spit with Casey, I accidentally stepped on a worm. With the Australian heat and bushland come so many animals that fly, crawl, or slide. There are centrepedes, cockroaches, earth worms, witchety grubs, moths, spiders, stick insects, wasps, and flies everywhere.

I hate being in a room, happily doing my thing, and looking up to the ceiling to see an enormous intruder of a spider. I'm ruthless and I don't care about life. I lunge for the vacuum cleaner and hoover it up. I used to go for the broom, but in my terrified clumsiness, after whacking it, the spider would fall on top of me. I would have a complete melt-down and do a panicked dance, giving the spider a chance to run, and we would spend the next half hour playing hide and seek, and I would get angry.

My Mosman neighbour, Johno, always said, 'If you ever need anything, you know where I am.'

I needed Johno desperately one evening. I got into bed, ironically making myself as snug as a bug, when I heard a noise in the darkness. Scuttle, scuttle, scuttle. I froze and listened. Scuttle, scuttle, scuttle. It was coming from the ceiling. I flicked on the lights. Sure enough, a giant brown cockroach was on the ceiling. Its legs were spread out and its antennas were moving back and forth, out of its ugly head. I dry-retched. With my hand over my mouth, I stifled my scream as I ran next door to Johno's front door.

'What's wrong?' Johno opened the door, dressed in shorts and a t-shirt.

Johno played rugby. He was of average height, with a big head, a thick neck, and a solid body. He was perfect for killing a cockroach.

'Please. Cockroach.'

With his thong in his hand, Johno followed me into my flat, to the bedroom. I pointed to the ceiling.

'Where?' said Johno, his eyes scanning the empty ceiling.

My eyes frantically searched the corners, the nooks, the crannies. My hands covered my mouth. I started hyperventilating, marching on the spot.

'Where?' repeated Johno.

I pointed to the ceiling, where nothing was. Johno looked at me with a frown. He walked around the room, looking in the corners. He banged his rubber thong on the wall. Nothing. He banged his thong on the floor. Nothing. He shook the curtains again and again. Nothing. Each time he banged, I was ready to flee, but the cockroach didn't come out. My nerves were shot. Johno looked at me. I was dressed in my pyjamas, which was a grey singlet dress with a cartoon mouse on the front.

Johno pointed. 'The only pest we have here is that one ya have on your breast, er, chest,' he joked, turning a bright shade of red.

I looked at him horrified. He sighed and took another look around the empty ceiling.

'I reckon he's disappeared outside, eh? We've made enough noise. He's gone.'

Johno walked towards the door. I grabbed his arm. He tried to shake my hand off. I tightened my grip, planted both my ankles into the carpet and anchored myself. Johno tried to move. I Chinese burnt his arm. He pulled again and I wouldn't let go.

Johno blushed at my attempts to keep him.

'Mica?' I stood my ground, my grip tightening on his arm.

'Let go.' He laughed gently as he prised my fingers, one by one, off his arm.

I stood, hyperventilating.

'He's gone. I promise,' said Johno, taking his thong and leaving.

Arming myself with a running shoe and a book, I circled that bedroom myself, searching for the intruder. Nothing. I pulled the sheets off my bed and flapped them about. Nothing. I shook the curtains again and again. Nothing. I tried a new approach.

'Thank you for leaving the flat,' I said aloud, whilst taking large breaths, in and out. 'Thank you. Goodbye and goodnight.'

After ten minutes, I walked over to the light switch with a

heavy sigh. As my hand reached for the switch, I heard it. Scuttle, scuttle, scuttle. I whipped around and looked up at the ceiling. There it was, on the ceiling, directly above my bed, above my fucking pillow! I screamed and threw the running shoe at the ceiling. It hit the cockroach, but it fell down onto my bed. I screamed and ran around in circles.

'Mica! Open!' Johno banged on the door.

I opened. 'On my bed!'

With his thong in his hand, he went straight for my bed. I stayed in the lounge room.

'Where are ya, ya bastard? There ya are!' Slam! Slam! Slam! 'Gotchya! You're a big one, aren't ya?'

I practised my breathing in the lounge room; long breath in, long breath out.

'It's okay!' he yelled. 'I killed him. I'll just grab a tissue from your bathroom. He's a bit squished.'

I dry-retched. 'Can you promise me he's dead?'

Johno came into the lounge, holding a tissue with brown cockroach legs sticking out. 'Yeah,' he said, holding the tissue up for me to see. 'He's as flat as a pancake, Mate!'

I turned my head away.

'I'll pop him in the bins outside. Okay then, you're okay now, he's gone. Goodnight.' Johno walked to the front door.

'Thank you. Goodnight.' I closed the door and leant against it.

I took deep breaths, my eyes looking towards the bedroom. I put my hand up to my hair, sure I would find a million grey hairs in the morning.

After checking and double-checking the fly-screens on all the windows and doors, I stripped my bed and pillows, and put everything in the washing machine. Finally, with fresh sheets on the bed, and Versace sprayed on both wrists, I laid down in the dark, listening for noises. Nothing. I listened some more. Nothing. Nerves shot to pieces, I lay and tried to calm my mind, but I kept having the same thoughts, "Oh, this country. Too many fucking cockroaches."

When I was an English teacher, I taught a lot of Brazilian students. They like Australia because it is geographically similar to their country, in places. Both countries have long stretches of beautiful beaches. In Brazil, however, you can swim in the sea with much less care, apparently. In Australia, you never know what you're getting into each time you step in the water. It's a game of chance. Will nothing happen? Or will you see a dolphin? Or a shark? A crocodile, if you're in the north? Will you be sucked out to sea by the strong current? Will you get stung by a jellyfish, or two? At the same time, will the searing sun burn your skin so badly you won't be able to lie on your back for the next three days? Ah, the game of chance for an inexperienced beach-goer in Oz!

As a kid, my family always took our summer holiday at a family beach resort called Bribie Island. One of the fun parts of the holiday was going to the Surf Club for a meal. The food is more sophisticated now, but when I was growing up, the Surf Club had lots of what I loved, and that was batter. Beer-battered fish, battered prawns, and battered potato scallops. It was deep-fry paradise. My body wanted oil and lots of it. It also wanted sliced white bread with butter, just give me more, more, more! And Coca-Cola too!

Australia has a high obesity rate for children, and it is not surprising. Without trying to be too Maria-Louisa about it, I had noticed on my return, how large the food portions were, compared to France. What Australians consider a normal portion of fries, to me, was a super-size portion. I'm not sure the super-size portions existed when I was a kid, but if they did, I was having it. I was having everything, except the salad.

My Salvadorian mother never missed an opportunity to put us kids to work, even on holidays. While other kids played on the beach, Mango, Beebee, and I had to work on the beach. We had to stand by the water's edge, feet apart, and swivel. We'd swivel down deep into the sand till we found clams. We had a bucket, and it was our job to fill that bucket. Swivel, swivel, work, work. What was my mother doing? She was up on the beach, on the picnic blanket, enjoying a beer, and chatting to everyone in her broken English. We were not allowed to complain. Her logic was, "You find the clams, and I cook the clams." Lucky for us, we were excellent clam-finders, so afterwards, we did get loads of fun time in the water.

It wasn't much fun for me one particularly sunny day, however. I was six years old. I wore my blue bikini with the little pink flowers, and my goggles. I went into the water laughing, and I came out screaming. I stood on the beach crying until a woman came to help. I couldn't see anything because my long hair was draped across my goggles. My body was burning. The lady made me stand still and somehow picked jellyfish off my arms, stomach, and the tops of my legs. She lay me down on the sand and told me to relax, while the other adults who'd gathered had a conversation.

'Vinegar's supposed to be good.'

'Yeah, but who's got vinegar?'

'You can pee on it, that's supposed to help.'

'Yeah. I'm not going to pee on her.'

'Nah, I'm just saying.'

'Yeah, I know.'

'Put wet sand on her.'

'Yeah. OK.'

I lay in a sand tomb, and after a while, I stopped crying. The adults asked me if I was alright.

I sat up. 'I'm going to go and find my Mum.'

'Okay, Sweetheart.'

When I reached my family much further along the beach, they were setting up food on the blanket.

'Go and wash out these plates and cups please,' said my sister, seeing me approach.

I stood for a second, but nobody looked at me, or noticed the red welts on my skin.

My mother said, 'Hurry up.'

I hurried up the beach to the water tap, lightly touching my welts as I went. When I got back, we ate prawn and mayonnaise sandwiches. My sister studied the prawn in her sandwich intently.

'Is that little black line, poo?' She took a half-eaten prawn out of her sandwich and held it up to study it.

'Just eat it,' my mother said.

Evidently, my mother by this stage had adapted to the Australian lifestyle by giving us those white bread sandwiches. Real sandwiches, just like all the other families on the beach. I munched away, but internally I was planning a rather big revenge involving sticks, on some jellyfish.

It seems my sister had a thing for foods of the sea because years later, as an adult, she ended up becoming the manager of a Fish and Chip shop. The shop was situated on a quiet beach where fishermen brought in fresh catches daily. Mango gutted and cleaned the fish, and the team cooked it and sold it. It was physical work and Mango loved it. She went home happy, and each evening, she leant in for a kiss from her husband, Andrew.

Each evening, ever-tactful Andrew said, 'You stink.'

Mango always shouted, 'I do not stink! You stink!'

When I visited Mango at her work one day, years before I left for London, we took a cigarette break, outside by the jetty. She brought a bag of fish cut-offs.

'Why?' I asked, looking at the bag in her hand.'For the pelicans.'

These pelicans were like her pets. Over-sized and cumbersome, they flew in to gather around my sister. She started throwing fish pieces. Greedy and speedy seagulls descended from out of nowhere.

'Get away!' I waved my hands about and kicked my legs.

'Oh Mica, they're only saying hello.'

'They are scavengers and persistent and annoying.'

'You never did know how to share,' said my sister gently, throwing a piece of fish to a patient pelican.

Midway through my Sydney university year, Mango flew down to visit me in Mosman. I hadn't seen her in years and it was so very wonderful to hug her again. She had put on a little weight, and her black hair was really long. She wore it in a single thick plait. I left her the keys to the flat whilst I went to university each day.

One evening, my neighbour Johno stopped me by the bins.

'Ya got visitors, eh?'

'Yes!' I smiled brightly.

'All the way from China, eh?'

'Pardon?'

'The short fat Chinese lady?' said Johno, throwing his rubbish in the communal bin. 'Yeah, she's friendly, she's smiled at me a couple of times.'

With my mouth wide open, I went back into my flat. Mango was in the kitchen, having a coffee and shoving a piece of cake in her mouth. She smiled at me and her eyes went kind of crinkly.

'Johno thinks you're a short fat Chinese lady,' I said, doubling over in laughter.

Her face fell. She didn't have a clue what I was talking about.

'What?'

Through my laughter and tears, I explained, and Mango avoided Johno for the rest of the week.

I had an afternoon free from university classes. I wanted to do something stress-free with my sister.

'Meet me at the aquarium this afternoon. I haven't been yet, and it's supposed to be a good one.'

'Okay,' said Mango.

When my morning classes finished, I packed up my papers alongside my two twenty-year-old friends.

Young Maiden said, 'What are you wearing tomorrow?'

Blondie said, 'I've got this skirt, but it's a bit short.'

'Wear it.'

'Yeah, and I've got these awesome stilettos to go with it. What are you wearing, Mica?'

'Clothes. Goodbye.' I shoved the last of my papers into my bag and left.

I met my sister outside the aquarium. 'Did you see Johno

on your way out?' I teased.

'I'm not that fat.' She shook her head in offence.

I love aquariums. I like watching things glide, and I like looking at pretty things like flat peaceful Angelfish. Mango and I flitted from fish tank to fish tank, and soon Mango began to impart her expertise.

'That one there, you only cook for a minute on each side,' she said, pointing.

We walked along to the next tank.

'That one, too many bones, don't bother.'

She was never one for tact, something she shares in common with her tea-drinking, deaf husband.

Mango's perception of fish, and what they exist for, gave me a horrific flashback to my childhood. My mother called for me in the back garden when I was little. I ran to her.

'Catch the duck. Quick!'

'My duck?'

'Si!' she nodded fervently.

Stupidly, I caught the duck and took it to her. Next thing I knew he was hanging, headless, upside down on the damn clothesline. That evening, I saw him again, on the kitchen table.

In the aquarium, my sister continued, 'Octopus. Really easy to cook. You got to whack him around a bit first, chop his head off, get his guts out, peel his skin, and cook him! Very high temperature and only for a minute or so.'

I watched the slow-moving octopus in his fish tank.

'What about eels?' I said to my sister.

'What?'

'Bet you don't know how to catch an eel in the mud.'

She looked at me, her long black plait hanging from her head.

'I do,' I said, walking off, laughing to myself.

Mango had a good week with me. We did lots of things. We took my chartered ferry over to Circular Quay and had coffee and cake at The Rocks. We visited Bondi Beach and also Manly. We walked up my hilly street to have focaccias in Oooorstraaarliyah Mosman, before walking past my place of work.

'Two hundred dollars for a teddy bear?' Mango's eyebrows rose as she looked at the window display.

I nodded.

'Two hundred dollars!' she repeated.

I took her to China Town for a meal on her last evening. It seemed only appropriate. She did, unknowingly, get her own back at me though. As we walked through the brightly coloured mall with dangling red lanterns, we walked past a lesbian couple holding hands.

Mango said, 'We've got those in Brisbane.'

'You've got what? People?'

'Ladies.'

'Ladies who like ladies?'

'Yeah, you know.' She looked embarrassed.

I suddenly felt mean. 'Yes. I know.'

I gave Mango a big reassuring smile. I felt regret for trying to make her say 'Lesbians'. I know my family is challenged when talking about subjects like homosexuality, drugs, and sex. We are behind in our maturity. Yet, I love my Mango, with all my heart, and she loves me and I had just tried to change her, and that made me feel mean.

As we strolled through China Town, we passed a heavily pregnant woman. I must have sighed as I looked at her, cause Mango rubbed my arm and said, 'Don't worry Mica, one day you'll get your fella.'

I considered it might be the opportune time to tell her about Dot. I hated the thought of her finding out second-hand about my girl relationship. She would feel betrayed by me. I looked up at her happy Chinese face and pushed the thought away. It was long over. Why would she ever find out?

Chapter 11

Moira and Elisa came to my place for coffee and they brought the dog with them.

'Whatever happened to Dot?' they asked.

'She came out to her family. She told me in an email.' I placed an Oooorstraaarliyah Custard Brioche from the bakery up the road, on the table.

'Wow. When are you going to come out to your family?' Elisa asked, sipping her coffee.

'Not funny.' I pinched her nose. 'Help yourselves.' I pushed the brioche towards them.

In my emails with Dot, I had kept my tone light, with lots of "I'm fine, Mate." Dot had thankfully remained behind her emails and text messages. She hadn't, as I'd feared, shown up on my doorstep.

Halfway through my Sydney year, she sent me an email that made my mouth drop open.

'I've met someone.'

I grabbed the screen with both hands, eyes scanning for more information.

'She's a lawyer.'

Lawyer? Wow, I read on.

'She's younger than me.'

Younger? I was older. I nodded. I read on.

'She's tall, thin, and has long blonde hair.'

Tall, thin, blonde? And a young lawyer. Okay. Okay. I nodded. Alright. Alright. This is excellent news.

I stood up, stretching my body. I stretched my arms out left and right, as far as they would go. I rolled my head around and around, feeling bits of negative energy flow out of me.

Jumping back into my seat, I grabbed the computer and typed. 'I'm really happy you have a girlfriend! You deserve to be happy and loved.'

Dot's new relationship enabled us to open up our conversations, and over the next days of writing back and forth, I rediscovered the funny girl I had met back in London.

'I'm sorry I was a stalker to you,' she said, in a reply later that week.

'Yes. You were.'

'It's thanks to you that I am so happy with my new girlfriend.'

'Is it?'

'Yes. We both said we were never relationship-type people. But I learnt, with you, that I am a relationship person.'

I had visions of her walking down the aisle with this new girlfriend. Chained together, forever.

'That's great,' I said.

'And you? You must be happy in your relationship too?'

I looked around my empty studio, my pillows sitting in the middle of my bed.

'Yes, all good here, Mate.' I typed, logging out of my email and once again, taking a long happy breath.

I looked at my computer screen for ages, with my empty coffee cup coffee next to it. I started humming, 'Congratulations, and hhhmm-hhhmm-ations'. My head nodded in time to the music in my head, and I waved an imaginary orchestral wand. I clapped my hands. 'Bravo!' I said to my studio, jumping around in circles.

Dot finding new love was the final chapter in this ridiculous drama. Over and out. And my family never found out! Yoo-hoo! I lifted my hands up to the heavens and quoted Alanis, 'Thank you India!'

After Mr Blond Dreads in London, I stopped having one-night stands. I had finished with the twelve-hour maximum deals. Not because I wanted to be kinder and more respectful to myself, nor because I had finally matured and understood it might be time for me to look for a long-term relationship with a guy. It also wasn't because I had come to any particular realisations about being gay or not. True, after my dinner party with my lesbian friends, Moira and Elisa, I still remained attracted to Elisa, but that was an admirative attraction, not a proper girl attraction. I stopped having one-night stands because, the dame herself, Mother Nature, stepped in with a helping hand.

'What is it?' I asked the doctor.

'Just a little cyst. Has it been there long?' he leant in for a closer look.

'Ten months now, and it's growing bigger.' I frowned. 'It's not anything sexually transmitted, is it?'

The doctor laughed. 'No. It's not. You can leave it or get it cut out if you like. Up to you.'

'Cut it out.'

That evening I told my friend, Casey.

'Show me,' she said.

I poked my tongue out.

She laughed. 'A wart on your tongue!'

My face flushed. 'It's a cyst, thank you very much, and it's getting cut out.'

'When?'

'I don't know, I'm waiting for a letter from the hospital.'

'Proper surgery? For a little wart?'

'Cyst.'

'Whatever. Very sexy.'

I pulled the neck of my t-shirt up over my head. 'I know! I'm hideous!'

Unbelievably, it would be this polyp on my tongue which would straighten out the straight girl in me.

Six weeks later, I sat in the waiting room of the Ear, Nose, and Throat ward, rubbing my cyst against my top lip. I looked around at the other patients in the waiting room. They had made an effort to come to hospital. They wore clothes that matched and proper shoes. I looked down at my faded t-shirt, worn jeans, and old running shoes. I didn't even have any make-up on. I had brushed my hair at least. I smoothed it down and sat up straight.

'Mica Maloney?' A nurse called.

I stood, smoothed down my old jeans, and followed her into a room where she asked me to fill in a load of forms.

'The doctor will be with you shortly, Mica.'

According to my appointment letter, it was a certain Dr Patel.

I studied the room. There was a mobile stretcher bed to the side. Is that where Dr Patel was going to stand when he put a huge needle into my tongue? This was going to be painful. I inhaled my N°5 wrists. More painful would be going through life with a cyst on my tongue.

The door opened and a tall, young doctor with light brown curly hair walked in. He wore a long white overcoat, opened at his bare chest, and baggy hospital work pants. I looked at his round, soulful eyes and then down to his bare chest, then back to his round eyes. He looked at my eyes. He didn't smile.

He held out his hand. 'I'm Jayd. Jadyon.' He spoke with a New Zealand accent.

I shook his hand. I looked at his chest again. He had chest hair. I looked back to his face.

'Take a seat,' he said, taking a swivel chair for himself,

and wheeling himself to sit right in front of me.

He picked up my papers and read. He looked at me, still not smiling. I remained frozen, unable to smile either.

'Okay, let's have a look,' he said.

I poked out my tongue and he leant in. My damn eyes went straight for that chest. What was wrong with me? I looked up at him. His round, brown eyes were looking straight back.

My heart was in a flutter, and perhaps his was too, because he said, 'Nee llbbps ooo bmmmps?'

'Pardon?' I frowned.

He self-corrected within a split second. 'Any lumps or bumps?'

I had no idea what he was referring to. The doctor leant in, his face very close to mine. His chest was thirty centimetres away. He reached towards me. His hands went for my hair, which hung loosely over my shoulders. I sat absolutely still, too scared to breathe. With his hands on either side of my neck, he slowly pushed my hair back over my shoulders, first the right side, then the left. I stared at him, aware of my breathing. His eyes were still on me, he was about twenty-five centimetres away. With a hand on either side of my neck, his fingers touched my collarbones, then pressed into the sides of my neck. He started massaging. I stared at him. He stared at me. Twenty-five short centimetres. His fingers massaged their way up to my jawline. I could barely breathe, I was going to pass out. He stopped, slowly took his hands away and leant back. His eyes stayed on mine. Still no smile.

'No lumps or bumps.'

I blew out an enormous sigh.

Dr Brown Eyes scribbled notes in my file.

'The procedure is fairly straightforward. It will be me who does the op.'

I finally found my voice. 'Do you think it's contagious?'

He shook his head.

'I haven't kissed anyone in ten months,' I said.

He leant forward. 'You haven't kissed anyone in ten months?'

I nodded, staring into his eyes.

'Well, no, it's not contagious. You could kiss someone,' he nodded towards the corridor, 'in the theatre, if you wanted.'

I mentally slid out of my chair and onto the floor.

He quickly joked, 'Not that you know anybody in the theatre.'

I laughed awkwardly and my eyes went for the chest again. What was wrong with me? My heart was going bananas.

The doctor stood up, so I stood up.

'Your surgery is scheduled for this afternoon. A nurse will take you to a waiting room. I'll see you shortly.'

He walked me out of the room and handed me over to a

nurse.

'Do you mind if I use the bathroom?' I asked the nurse.

She pointed to the end of the corridor and I ran to the bathroom, straight to the mirror.

Number One took one look. "Aaaaagh! You're hideous!"

I dived into my handbag, pushing aside used tissues, old bits of paper with scribbled shopping lists, and at least a dozen pens. At the bottom, I found a mascara stick. I took it out and ripped off the lid. With shaky hands, I put mascara on my lashes. Then I pinched my cheeks until they turned pink. Fuck! I brushed my hair with my fingers and looked at myself in the mirror.

Number One panicked alongside me. "Why, oh why, didn't you make an effort this morning? WHY?"

An hour later, the nurse poked her head in the door.

'Miss Maloney?'

I sat up on my hospital bed, every single hair on my head was in place.

The nurse placed a gown on my bed and some throwaway operation underpants. 'Take off all your clothes and put these on. Take off all jewellery too. You can leave your shoes on.'

I stood in front of the mirror and looked at myself, wearing a tablecloth garment which opened at the back. On my feet, I wore grey socks and my old, dirty running shoes. I was about to go in to have surgery with a most intriguing doctor, and I hadn't even waxed my legs. I had short black stubby hairs growing on my legs, and my tablecloth gown wasn't floor-length.

'Miss Maloney? Follow me.'

The nurse and I walked into a very spacious fluorescent-lit theatre, with a chaise longue type operation table in the middle of it. Two young female nurses, with green masks over their faces, walked around, picking up and putting down utensils. In the corner of the grand room, an older guy sat in front of a computer.

'Hello Mica. I'm Dr Patel,' he called to me as I walked in.

'Hello,' I replied, standing in my tablecloth.

In the middle of the room stood "my doctor", with his soulful eyes and chest. He wore a green mask over his mouth. He stood by the chaise longue. We made eye contact. He nodded towards the chaise longue. I walked over and lay down, biting my bottom lip.

When I first saw the original GP doctor regarding my cyst, and he told me I could have it cut out, I hadn't really thought about my low pain threshold. I imagined they could put some cream on my tongue to make it numb before putting a needle in.

'No,' said the nurse earlier today, when I had asked. 'To make it numb, you need to have a needle into your tongue.'

'No cream first?'

'No. That's the needle's job.'

'A needle straight into my tongue, with no cream?'

She looked at me square in the eyes. 'The tongue is a muscle. It's going to hurt.'

One of the young nurses in green masks came over, holding black material.

'I'm going to wrap your head and eyes, Mica.'

Surprised, my eyes went to Dr Soul Eyes. He was standing right beside me. The nurse wrapped my bewildered head and made a little turban, and covered my eyes too, leaving my nose free to breathe. She pushed me to lie back on the chaise longue and I heard her walk away. The darkness, and the tight fit of the turban, was a good technique. It took away some panic, but not all. My breathing accelerated and my chest moved up and down. I felt Dr Soul Eyes' palm press firmly down on my chest. I stopped breathing. When I couldn't hold my breath any longer, I started breathing again. His palm pressed firmly on my chest and it stayed there till my breathing regularised.

'I'm going to put the needle in now, Mica,' said my young doctor.

I lay still. Once injected, we waited a few minutes for the anaesthetic to work.

He said, 'Feel that?'

I shook my turban.

It wasn't long afterwards that the operation was over and the nurse was unwrapping my turban. I blinked and looked around for Dr Soul Eyes. He was over in the corner, putting his tools away.

'Okay?' the nurse asked.

I nodded. My tongue felt like the size of a balloon.

'Alright,' continued the nurse, 'that's you done. You can go. Nurse Marie will take you back to get changed.

Chief Doctor Patel spoke from the corner. 'We'll send you a letter in a few weeks. We'll have the results of the biopsy, but the procedure went fine and it all looks good.'

Dr Soul Eyes stood on the other side of the room.

I opened my mouth to speak. My swollen tongue got in the way. 'Doctha?'

He looked at me.

'Ttttthhhhank thoo.'

I walked out wearing my tablecloth, throwaway knickers, and dirty trainers. I was minus one wart but plus one amazing attraction experience. It threw me. I would never doubt my straightness again, or even think I might be a half lesbian. I had such a strong desire to get physically close to this man. My loins were yearning, they were actually yearning. I had never felt that for a woman. What I had felt was curiosity, and in my dramatic fashion, I took that curiosity, added in self-doubt and my negative beliefs about men, to create a fantastic cocktail of different beliefs about myself. Things were crystal clear now, and I was well and truly awoken. Hallelujah Soul Eyes!

The hospital was on the south side of Sydney, so after the check-up, I went for a long walk along the cliffs from Bondi towards Bronte Beach. I knew the path well. Many moons ago, when I was first studying at university, for this very degree that I was now completing, I worked part-time as a waitress in a coffee shop on Bondi Beach. The coffee shop window sold made-on-the-premises strudels of every sort, rich forest cakes, super-sized macarons, gooey mud cakes, giant rum balls, and creamy custard slices. Tourists hovered around the display window for ages, drooling.

I worked with a glamorous Russian manager who wasn't shy to express herself. She hated the way I wore my uniform. My top was too loose and my black pants were too baggy.

'What's this, darling?' She pulled at my baggy pants. 'Tighter pants, darling! Please!'

The other waitresses, mostly Hungarians and Russians, wore tight tops and pants, and they got good tips, though they were also very good at their jobs. I didn't do too badly, baggy pants and all.

These Bondi Beach Coffee Shop days were funny days, madly running between tables serving lattes and strudels to tourists in bikinis and thongs, the foot kind. I spent a lot of time laughing with my co-worker Linda, who was the only other Australian. We laughed constantly, often at the cultural differences between the staff.

The Hungarians never understood our sense of humour. 'What are you crazy bitches laughing about this time?'

I started my Bondi cliff walk, in the direction of Tamarama. I was only three minutes along the cliff path, when I stopped to look down to the Bondi Surf Club seawater pool. It was impressive. The full-length pool was built into the sea, and waves from the open sea crashed over the side, pouring into the pool. An old man laboriously swam his laps up and down, in the rocking seawater. The crashing waves had no effect on him and he continued to place one strong arm in front of the other, pulling his sturdy body along. I stood, mesmerised in the open air, watching from above.

A man came past me on the cliff path. I moved forward to let him pass and out of the corner of my eye, I caught something white, grey, and furry. I turned to look and saw the head of a ferret over his shoulder. Shaking my head, I looked back down to the sea pool.

"Hello," said Number Two, "two very fit lifesaver dudes."

Two young guys with triangular bronzed bodies walked along the side of the pool, getting ready to join the old man. I unconsciously touched my tongue where the cyst had been.

Number One said, "Less perve, more walk please."

I moved my body along the path, with my head held high, facing the open sea. The sea breeze played with my loose hair, like Dr Soul Eyes had, gently pushing it back. I slowly inhaled the cleansing sea air. My body sensed a change in me. I was becoming ready for another romance, with a guy. I could feel it.

Chapter 12

The end of the year was fast approaching. My bank statement lay on the dining table and it stated, "You are a flat-broke motherfucker."

Scratching the back of my neck, I opened my computer and checked flights to France. Then I checked flights to London. I pictured Marilyn and Cristal at the airport, with open arms and alcoholic reunion plans. I looked at the bank statement again. My shoulders slumped. I ran my cyst-less tongue across my top teeth, stared at the computer, and decided to look at a website for English Language Teachers. There was a job being offered at Manly beach. I liked the thought of going for a swim during lunchtime, at the surf side. I typed out an application letter.

Dear Sir/Madam

I'm writing to apply for the job as English Language Teacher, as seen advertised on your website.

I have several years of experience teaching students of all nationalities and find that the Thai students are the best. The Brazilians are the most fun, but do they really enjoy grammar lessons? We all know they'd much prefer to be at the beach with a barbecue. Who wouldn't? The Japanese students are at ease with the grammar lessons, but do they find it easy to do silly speaking activities, which require you to make a fool of yourself in front of others? Not so easy. Thai students on the other hand, even though they face some pronunciation challenges, are the ideal mix of fun and study. Thai and Colombian (have you ever noticed how all Colombians have magnificent teeth? Generally speaking of course, eh!)

I wouldn't want to leave out the Saudis. I taught one entrepreneur, his level was beginner, but he wasn't beginner in social skills. He asked me for my telephone number and I said, "You're a beginner. What are you going to say to me on the telephone?" He put a pretend phone up to his ear, and said, "Hello, hello, hello." I thought this showed great potential and didn't want to put him off his English progress. As I gave him my number, my cheeky Spanish student said, "Wife number two." In any case, it is for this reason I cannot dismiss those fun Saudis too. Put them in with the Thais and the Colombians. Go on, throw in the Spanish too.

However, I digress. I am currently working in a maternity clothing boutique. This is part-time and very shortly I will need to be working full-time, once my university studies finish, because the wine is expensive in Australia. Hopefully, the fact that I returned to university as a mature-age student demonstrates an incredible lack of foresight on my part, considering I was living a paradisiac lifestyle just prior, in the South of France and it hadn't occurred to me that I might have been able to complete a degree there. My current part-time maternity job has been rewarding but challenging as I've had to pretend to be trying to get pregnant each shift. Pretending is one of my strengths you should note. My weaknesses may be that I like to stereotype a lot, and I seriously lack the ability to communicate maturely. It is for these reasons I believe I would make an excellent language teacher.

Thank you for your time and consideration. I look

forward to hearing from you.

I got the job and started immediately. My first day at the language school in Manly, I called the register.

'Diego?'

'Here.'

'Anna Rosa?

'Here, Miss.'

'Caterina?'

'Here.'

'Alfonso?'

'Here, Teacher.'

I looked up. Half the class had that very relaxed look about them.

'Who are the Brazilians?' I asked.

Half the class raised their hands, big happy smiles on their gorgeous faces. I nodded, understanding at once. If you were a Brazilian student studying English, which language school were you going to choose? The one by the beach and the barbecues. Using my previous teaching experience, I put a new rule in place because I'd had far too many Brazilian students give me the same reason for being late for class before.

'Sorry Teacher, my mother...,' a student would come

bursting into class late, making a telephone sign with his hand.

'Yes, it's always your mother.'

I instilled my new rule. 'Starting tomorrow, if you are more than fifteen minutes late, you have to sing a song in front of all of us.'

Faces fell across the room as the Koreans and Japanese got visibly anxious at the prospect of making a fool of themselves in public. They didn't like it.

The next day when the Slovakian student was late, he really didn't like it. 'Please. No.' He begged as he came in sixteen minutes late.

'Go on,' I said. 'It can be anything, a nursery rhyme if you like.'

Standing in the middle of the room, with head bowed, arms folded in front, he started to sing in his wobbly voice, 'Dobrú noc má milá,...'

For the most part, this was an effective method, except when it came to the Brazilians. The day Diego was late, he came bursting into the room, saying 'Sorry Teacher, my mother...'

'You know the rule, sing your song.'

A happy smile spread over Diego's face and he positioned himself smack bang in the middle of the room. He was dressed for the beach, wearing thongs, boardshorts, and a sleeveless t-shirt. The Korean girls' eyes went to the tattoos on his strong bare arms, and they smiled at him.

Standing tall, Diego looked around at his fellow students. 'Okay!' he said, starting to clap his hands, 'come on everyone, clap your hands!'

His energy was infectious, and we had an impromptu lesson on Brazilian folk songs.

In my Mosman studio, the phone rang.

'Hello?'

'Hi, it's me,' my sister said.

'Hey! Are you excited?'

'Yeah, but a bit busy. I ordered the pig today.'

'Good. Let me know if there is anything I can do from this end.'

'Nothing. It's all organised, Mica. You just need to get here. What about you? Are you excited? Today is your last day, isn't it?'

'You said it! God, I can't believe after all these years of talking about it, that I did actually come back, and I finished it.'

'I'm proud of you.'

'Thanks. I'm proud of myself. So, are you going to have enough space for this party or what?'

'I reckon just about. Everyone is coming. Except for BeeBee, which we knew cause it is too far for him to fly for just a weekend, and the boys are away too. But everyone else is coming. And Maria-Louisa is coming! I've got Andrew cleaning the back yard and the girls cleaning the house. Andrew's brother-in-law is going to help with the pig, and my work has given us a load of seafood.'

'Cool. Does Andrew know about his cake?'

We had ordered a cake for Andrew. Apparently, it was going to look just like a limousine.

'Nope. He's going to get a surprise. Er...,' Mango stopped.

I waited for her to finish her sentence. I held the phone to my ear, listening, but there was silence. Looking at my watch, I said, 'I've got to go Mango. I've got to hand in my last assignment.'

She laughed nervously. 'Oh! Okay, congratulations again!'

'Thanks! Bye!'

'Mica?' my sister's voice said.

'Yeah?'

'I love you, eh? Always remember that.'

'Yeah, me too. See you!' I hung up and grabbed my uni stuff.

I strode down to the ferry that morning, savouring each step as it would be my last university trip. The skies were blue, the sun was shining, and it was hot. I wore huge sunglasses to keep out the glare. My hair was piled in a knot on my head, to keep it from sticking to my patch-free neck. Cockatoos played above me, in and out of tall leafy trees. Down at the port, the water was sparkling, and the private boats were anchored, waiting to be taken out by their polo-shirt owners. I looked around and breathed in the tranquility.

I waited as the ferry putt-putted into the dock. About ten people were on board, ready to get off. My Japanese students had told me that in Tokyo, people are hired as people-pushers on their underground train platforms. Their job is to squash and push more people into the carriage, before the doors close. I looked at my situation. Here I was, waiting for the tenth person to get off, so I could walk the plank to go to my final university day. I peeked into my handbag, double-checking to see if the USB stick which held my last assignment was there. It was. I patted my bag and looked over into the clean Mosman water. I felt a sense of pride and accomplishment. I had really done it. I stood straight, breathed in the fresh air, and skipped up the plank.

'G'day!' said the ferryman, as I passed.

'Morning!' I smiled back.

A businessman followed me onto the ferry, holding his briefcase and a takeaway coffee from the coffee hut on the dock. What a super cool job that would be, working by the harbour, drinking as much coffee as you liked, eating posh little muffins, listening to the radio, and feeding the birds between ferry stops.

I sat on the upper deck to privately enjoy my sunshine. Seven minutes later, the pretty waterside suburbs of Cremorne Point and Kirribilli spread out before me, as we made our drop-offs and pick-ups.

Leaning back in my top deck seat, I thought back to my phone call with Mango. We were having a party at her house next week to celebrate Andrew's 50th birthday, and me finishing university. Everyone in my family would be there, except my brother and nephews. She had said Maria-Louisa would be there. Is that why Mango had said, "I love you, eh? Always remember that." Had Maria-Louisa said something? Had she even picked up on it, in the South of France?

"Let it go," said Number One. "It could be anything. You know what the family is like. Always some family drama going on."

All the family was going to the party; cousins, second cousins, and people who are introduced as cousins but who are not related in any way. Loads of people were coming and it was quite probable there was a new family drama, or two, that Mango didn't want to tell me about.

My mother had two sisters, Aunt Paloma and Aunt Lydia, or as I call her, Aunt Voodoo. Aunt Voodoo has four daughters; Dina, Delilah, Domenica, and Dallas. The Dirty D's. They are always together, whispering amongst themselves. Together with Aunt Voodoo, they move in unison, like a pack of hyenas, eyeing their prey from the outskirts, and sniggering and drooling. Maybe Mango knew some family drama about the Dirty D's? I shrugged the thought away. I shook my head about in the open air of the top deck, breathing in the glorious sunshine. I couldn't care who does what to whom, or who doesn't do what, to nobody.

I got off the ferry at Circular Quay, wearing my earphones and mouthing the words to 'Fat Bottomed Girls' as I swung my own fat bottom through Sydney centre. Businesswomen were wearing sleeveless linen dresses and strappy high heels, and businessmen were rushing past, wearing suits.

I walked towards university, stopping at Myers, a department store, on the way. I routinely stopped at their perfume department for a little squirt of Cartier, and a squirt of something new on the other wrist. Today it was Portofino by Dior. I sniffed both wrists as I walked out and continued to smell myself all the way to university.

Once out the front, I looked at the modern building where I had had my classes. I hadn't lost my bitterness or disappointment regarding university, but I had accepted that I had placed myself in this non-France situation. Taking in a deep sigh, I climbed those fucking stairs for the last time.

Mr Aussie Ocker saw me placing my assignment on his desk. 'Will we see you at graduation next May, Mica?'

'No.'

He picked up a huge Thank You card. 'Would you like to sign my card?'

I opened the card. The twenty-year-olds had written mini-essays, with declarations of gratitude for his fabulous regurgitation. They wrote of how he had changed their lives forever. Mr Aussie Ocker loitered.

I picked up a black pen and wrote, "All the best, Mica."

I waltzed out of the building and straight into the closest bottle shop.

'That'll be ten dollars and ninety-five cents please,' said the sales assistant. His baby-face, he couldn't have been much more than eighteen, contrasted with his body, which was strong and well-built.

'Thank you,' I said, shoving my champagne into my daypack.

With an appreciative smell of my wrists, I skipped towards Circular Quay.

Back on the other side of the harbour at Mosman jetty, I walked down the plank onto terra firma. A man, waiting to board, stood to one side to let me pass. I was wearing a navy blue and white striped maternity top. I was not only pretending to get pregnant, but I was walking around wearing sample maternity clothes. In my defence, the top is pretty, if a little suggestive because it displays my cleavage. The man's eyes went for my breasts and he muttered in his language, under his breath. It sounded like, "Harrak ma ella."

In my studio, I flung my uni bag into the corner like a frisbee and waltzed into the kitchen.

'Congratulations!' I said, pouring champagne into a coffee cup because I had broken my one wine glass the week before, running away from a spider.

'Why, thank you!' I accepted my own good wishes, bowing my head graciously. I tipped the bubbles down my throat.

My phone beeped, a text message from Melker. "Mica, where are you? We're at the harbour."

My university friends were already celebrating.

"Coming!" I texted, sticking a teaspoon in my champagne

bottle.

I sang to myself whilst I took a shower.

'I finished. I did it. I came back and aftertoomanyyearsofnotfinishingthedegree I fiiiiiiiiiinished. The degree is finished, that girl relationship is finished, my champagne is not finished.'

I decided to entitle that song, 'Finish'. Speaking of which, I had a Finnish waiting for me at the harbour.

My fellow mature-aged university friend, Melker, was born in Finland. He came complete with blue eyes and blond hair. He was waiting for me at the harbour to celebrate, along with Bottle-Blonde, Young Maiden, and the rest of our class. I put on my favourite jeans, another maternity top, and sprayed on some Must. Buckling the straps on my high-heeled sandals, I took one last look in the mirror before flying out the door with a big, happy, relieved, satisfied, and proud smile.

At the harbour-side bar, my student friends sat drinking at two long terrace tables overlooking the water.

'Hey, Mica! Over here!'

Excited twenty-year-old faces grinned over bottles of alcohol. It was the first time I had seen them outside of the university environment. At university they were loud, and here in this trendy city bar, they were getting louder with each sip.

'We did it!' they shouted.

Their young faces were cherubic and their happiness was contagious.

'We sure did!' I sat down next to Blondie.

Blondie had raided her mother's 70's wardrobe. She was wearing tight silver pants with silver heels, and a little black boob-tube. Her hair had been blow-dried Farrah Fawcett style. She looked like one of Charlie's Angels, in teenager form.

'I think I'm drunk already.' Blondie's words slurred.

I looked over at Young Maiden. She had a glass of something alcoholic in front of her. Her million eyelashes eyes saw me looking.

'I'm just going to sip it all afternoon and evening.'

'Good idea.' I thought back to Mosman jetty, and the admiring man. Young Maiden spoke Arabic. 'Does "Harrak ma ella," mean anything?' I tried my best to repeat the phrase correctly.

'Sounds a bit like, "Praise be to God."'

I smiled. 'Ah!'

Melker, my gay Finnish mate, came to my service. He called loudly, 'Champagne! Pass the bottle. Mica needs a champagne.'

Melker filled a glass, cleared his throat, and held the glass up so dramatically that the twenty-year-olds went quiet.

'Mica,' said Melker, holding my champagne glass high, 'all the best!'

The group burst out laughing. 'We saw the card!'

My classmates were so excited. I hadn't had the

opportunity to socialise with them outside of the university walls before, and didn't really know what they liked and disliked, or how they spent their leisure time. I listened to some of their conversations with my eyes widening.

'Join me in London,' said Alexia, grabbing her friend's arm.

Rachelle and Alexia had spent the university year sitting next to each other. They were complete opposites in looks. Alexia had light brown wavy hair and a round, sun-kissed, natural face. Rachelle had a pale face, wore blood-red lipstick, and lots of black eye-liner. Her hair was jet black and her straight fringe fell over her eyes.

When Rachelle heard Alexia invite her to London, she pouted. 'I can't, I have to start working in January, it's not fair!'

Tricia, the girl sitting opposite, asked, 'Have you found a job already?'

'Yes, my mother's best friend is a Marketing Director, and I'm going to work for her.'

'Wow!' said Tricia. 'You're so lucky.'

'Yes, but it means I can't hang out with Alexia in Europe.'

Rachelle grabbed Alexia's arm, and they clung to each other, like koalas.

Alexia suddenly sat up. 'Why don't you come for three weeks, before you start? Meet me in Florence.'

'No, we're going to Bali for three weeks. It's a family holiday. It's not fair!' Rachelle bowed her gothic head.

Blondie, Young Maiden and I looked on.

Dylan, sitting two seats down, said, 'Alexia, when you come back, you're going to be working across the road from me.'

Alexia smiled. 'We can have business lunches!'

Tricia's little face looked confused. 'Have you got a job already too?' she asked Alexia.

Alexia linked her koala arm with Rachelle. 'Yeah, my dad got me a job with Dylan's Dad's friend, who is a TV producer. I start when I get back from Europe.'

Tricia's eyes grew large. So did Blondie's, Young Maiden's, and mine.

'What's your job?' asked Tricia.

'Programme Researcher,' said Alexia.

'Wow!'

'Dylan got the better job, he's going to be Assistant Producer. It's not fair!' Alexia pouted. 'What's your job?'

'I don't have one yet,' said Tricia, shrinking back.

'Come to Europe with me!'

Tricia shook her curls. 'I can't afford it. How can you? Have you been working part-time?'

'No. My parents are paying. It's my gift for finishing university,' said Alexia. 'What did your parents get you?'

Tricia shook her head. 'Nothing.'

Rachelle's red mouth dropped open.

Alexia said, 'They could have at least bought you a car!'

Blondie, Young Maiden, and I gave each other the "Oh my God" look, and retreated back to our little group, abandoning poor Tricia, whose self-worth was diminishing by the second.

Blondie whispered, 'Man, I'm not going to Europe or getting a car, and I don't have a job lined up.'

Young Maiden said, 'It's not a race. Everyone goes at their own pace.'

Blondie bit her long red fingernail. 'What about you, Mica? What are you doing?'

'I'm going to Monte Carlo to be the Prince's personal media advisor because my dad knew his dad. I'll take board meetings on his yacht and sleep with gorgeous men who feed me truffles.'

The girls giggled.

I sat up straight. 'I'm teaching English until I can figure out how to get back to France.'

Blondie raised her glass. 'To us!'

Our class spent the rest of the afternoon and evening drinking, and repeating ourselves. The drunker we got, the shorter the time got between repeats.

'Thank God we finished that degree!'

'Thank fuck!'

'I never thought it would bloody end!'

'Never end!'

'I'm really fucking proud of us.'

'So proud.'

'I liked Mr Aussie Ocker,' exclaimed Tricia with a satisfied nod of her curls.

'He was alright.'

'He was nice.'

'I didn't appreciate his style,' I said, shrugging.

Melker placed his gorgeous Finnish arm around me and said, 'She fucking hated him! More champagne for Mica!'

In the evening, Melker took control of our little group. He was in the process of bundling us into a taxi. He had shouted to the remaining twenty-year-olds as we left, 'We're going to the Cross if anyone wants to join us!'

We didn't really need to continue the party as we were all, except for Young Maiden, totally drunk.

'I should go home. I can get the last train,' said Young Maiden.

'Get in the car.' Melker shoved her in the taxi. Blondie followed her in.

'Come on, Mica!' He shoved me in, and he got in after me. 'The Cross please, Driver!'

The bar looked like a private terrace house. It had a little paved courtyard out the front with mini trees covered in fairy lights. Music was playing inside, where people were standing by a long white bar. The clientele was a mix of young, beautiful people, immaculate in their tailored suits, and creative people in ripped jeans.

'My father is going to have a fit,' said Young Maiden.

Blondie tottered in a high heel, taking Young Maiden by her arm. 'No, he won't,' she slurred. 'He won't.'

'Shoe,' I said to Blondie as we stumbled forward and took a table in the paved courtyard.

Melker went inside to order drinks.

'Hmmmmm?' said Blondie.

'Where's your other shoe?'

Blondie only wore one high-heeled silver shoe. 'Oh!' she said, 'I don't know.'

Melker arrived with the drinks, nearly falling and spilling the drinks on us.

I fell into my standard alcohol-driven behaviour of talking non-stop.

'You're going to be a magnificent PR person, Melker,' I said, patting his chest.

Melker placed his arm around me and he leant in and gave me a nudgey peck on my cheek. Then a peck on my lips. 'How come you're so beautiful, hhmmmmm?' Melker nibbled my cheek and looked down my maternity top.

Number One was in a bit of shock. "You're going for the

gay man? Seriously?"

Number Two jumped in. "Relax Max, it's called having fun."

I looked at Melker's face. He was so perfect, with his angelic blond hair, blue eyes, strong jawline, and naughty smile. His lips were perfect. My lips touched his perfect lips, and we kissed slowly. His hands went around my patch-free neck, pulling me close. I closed my eyes, enjoying the feel of his lips pressing on mine.

Melker didn't close his eyes. 'Excuse me, Darling,' he said, pushing me back suddenly. His lovely blue eyes had focussed on a young, tall, well-dressed man who had just walked in.

With my lips still pursed for kissing, I watched Melker follow Mr Tall, Dark, and Handsome inside the bar.

'Where's Melker going?' slurred Blondie.

'Aaaaay yay yay.' A wry smile spread across my face. 'You win some, you lose some.'

'Huh?'

'Huh?'

'What? No, I asked you. Oh, never mind.' Blondie waved away the idea. She sat with her thin legs crossed, and swung her shoe-less foot back and forth. 'Vodka?' She lifted the bottle towards me.

I waved my finger. 'I don't think I can do it.'

This was the last thing I remember saying that night.

Somehow I got myself a taxi and went home, leaving them to continue the party. I know I left earlier than them, because at 4 a.m., lying in my bed, I got a text from Melker.

"Darling, where did you go? We're at the Cross. All the best. x"

I hoped he was successful in picking up Mr Tall, Dark, and Handsome.

I lay in bed wondering when my Tall, Dark, and Handsome would show up when suddenly, my toilet flushed. I sat up and gasped. Don't tell me I picked up? Oh my God! I looked over at the other side of my bed. My eyes went back to the bathroom door. It opened.

'My Dad's going to have a fit,' said a million eyelashes, walking past me, into my lounge.

I slipped out of bed and followed her, poking my head around the corner. I watched her lie down on a small makeshift bed on the floor. She snuggled up next to a lump. The lump had a Farrah Fawcett head. I tip-toed back to my bed, thinking, "Holy shit. Anyone else in here?"

"Darling, where did you go? We're at the Cross. All the best. x"

I hoped he was successful in picking up Mr Tall, Dark and Handsome.

I lay in bed wondering when my Tall, Dark and Handsome would show up when suddenly, my toilet flushed. I sat up and gasped. Don't tell me I picked up? Oh my God! I looked over at the other side of my bed. My eyes went back to the bathroom door. It opened.

'My Dad's going to have a fit,' said a million eyelashes, walking past me, into my lounge.

I slipped out of bed and followed her, poking my head around the corner. I watched her lie down on a small make-shift bed on the floor. She snuggled up next to a lump. The lump had a Farrah Fawcett head. I tip-toed back to my bed, thinking, "Holy shit. Anyone else in here?"

Chapter 13

I crawled out of bed at three in the afternoon, and stumbled to the fridge. 'No Coca-Cola. Damn.'

I shuffled into the lounge. There was a neat pile of bedding in the corner. I stared at it, frowning. I crawled over and saw a note.

"Thanks! Hope we didn't wake you. Have a great time in Brisbane with your family! Xx"

I stared back in the direction of the fridge and used all my energy to will Coca-Cola to appear. I willed and willed, from the lounge floor. I waited with severe bed hair and a drum solo playing in my head.

It was a long time before I got up to put some jeans on. I had a plan.

I stood outside McDonald's, holding my thumping head.

"Get in and get out," I told myself as I walked in and stood in the queue.

When it was my turn, a cheery teenager greeted me. Her bright eyes sparkled and her skin glowed. I was being served by the epitome of health.

'What can I get you?' Her perfect smile was genuine.

'Uhmmmm. Uhmmm. A Big Mac Meal with Coca-Cola please, large size.'

'Anything else?'

'Uhmmm, eeeeeer, a thickshake, strawberry please.'

'Anything else?'

'Errrrrr, yes, a chocolate sundae and a Double Cheeseburger meal, please.'

Holding bags of hot food, I tip-toed out of McDonald's back to the bus stop, whilst squinting.

Back at my place, I peeled off my jeans and put on enormous flannel pyjama pants. I sat on the lounge room floor, spreading my lukewarm grease feast around me.

I lay on the floor all afternoon, in a star shape, with empty McDonald's food papers strewn about, next to empty the paracetamol packet. My hand went up and rested on my right breast. 'Ooooh, harrak ma ella.' I managed a giggle.

I rolled onto my stomach and moved, caterpillar-style, to my desk. I dragged the computer onto the floor, and lay in front of it. Eventually, I turned it on. Emails, inbox, open. Email from Miss Dot. Hadn't heard from her in a while. Click, open.

'Mica, I have been tossing and turning for a couple of months now about whether or not to tell you. I have decided I should, as a courtesy to you. Your family know you're a lesbian.'

I blinked. I concentrated and re-read that last line.

'Your family know you're a lesbian.'

All the leftover alcohol evaporated in a split second as I started brewing a thunderstorm. I read on.

'I know you're going to hate me and I'm really sorry.'

My anger was coming from my gut and rising higher and higher. I continued reading.

'I worked with your cousin, Delilah. I didn't know she was your cousin. She said she was from Central America and I said my ex-girlfriend was from Central America. She said, "Who is she? I know all the Central Americans," and I said, "Nobody, forget it." But then the next day, she stopped me in the carpark and held up a photo of you. I got a big shock, and she said, "I knew it!"' I am so sorry.'

I lay on the floor, staring blankly at the ceiling. The blood fell from the top of my body down, almost into the floor. In disbelief, I looked back to the computer to re-read that first line.

'Mica, I have been tossing and turning for a couple of months now...'

A couple of months?

She continued her email.

'Delilah has promised to never tell anyone, and I believe her. I'm sorry this happened.'

I lay on the floor, looking to the ceiling, playing the movie in my head. Dirty Delilah is in her home, looking through old photo albums, trying to find a good one of me. Fast forward to her work carpark where she stands, waiting for Dot to finish work. Dot strolls through the carpark. Delilah lunges forward, thrusting a photograph of me into Dot's face. Dot gasps. Dirty Delilah grins and runs back to her sniggering hyena pack.

Fast forward again, Delilah is at a family barbecue talking

to my sister.

'How's Mica?' Delilah asks.

'Great,' replies Mango.

'Still single?'

'Yep. But she'll find her fella one day.'

'Do you think so?' laughs Delilah.

'Yes,' says my sister. 'Why?'

'No reason,' says Dirty D walking off, smiling smugly to her knowing sisters and mother.

I breathed long, loud, deep breaths.

'Aaaaaaaaarrrrrrrrrrrrrrrrrrggggggghhhhh!'

My nails dug deep, scratching the itchy psoriasis patch on my arm. I scratched until I drew blood. I looked to my suitcase, ready to be packed to go to Brisbane. I began ripping my fingernails. The skin under my nails bled, and yet I still tried to scratch my psoriasis patch. I thumped the carpet again and again and again. I went to the bathroom and vomited. Exhausted, I turned on the hot water, crawled in and sat on the shower floor. The burning water rained over my body. I sat, motionless, under the pouring heat as my skin got redder and redder.

When I finally lay down in bed that evening, I felt calmer. I looked up at my ceiling. There was no cockroach in sight. I gave a weak smile. Talking out loud, I said, 'This isn't the end of the world. I can and will, handle it. This isn't the end of the world. Keep perspective.'

I woke up the next day and remembered I'd finished university. I smiled. Then I remembered my family thinks I'm a lesbian. Hot anger rose up through my body. Getting out of bed, I stretched, determined to remain in control. I put the coffee on, then went to the bathroom and took out a bandage. I wrapped my raw psoriasis patch. I put bandaids on my fingers, where the nails were so short it hurt. Back in the living room, I turned on the computer. It beeped and whirred. Outside, it was a glorious Sydney summer day. Birds chirped loudly in the trees by my kitchen window. Happy blue skies and happy birds did not make me happy. I typed my reply.

'Dot, I can't believe you've known for months without telling me. I wish I had never met you. I hate you. You make me sick. Mica.'

I went outside to my smoking step. By the end of the morning, my ashtray resembled a little ash temple, with cigarette butts circling it protectively.

At midday, still dressed in my pyjamas, I took the opened champagne bottle with the teaspoon sticking out, and poured myself a mug. I drank and stared at the birds, flitting between branches. I had another cigarette on my step and the last mug of champagne before finally picking up the phone and dialling.

'Hello?' Mango's husband answered the phone.

'Hi Andrew. It's me.'

'Yeah, we heard something about you,' he said in his lazy Australian drawl.

Andrew is a builder. He likes cars, trucks, and dogs. He

eats jam sandwiches and hamburgers whilst standing up, and he drinks cold cups of tea. He smokes, and he talks loudly because he is going deaf.

I put my champagne mug down.

Andrew said, 'Yeah, the family reckon you're gay,' and as if I needed help with the definition, he added, 'that you like girls.'

I closed my eyes as I tried to understand that this was actually happening.

'Well? Do you?' continued my tactful brother-in-law.

'No. Is Mango there please?'

I went inside and lay on my carpet, taking the phone with me.

'Hey ya!' Mango came on the phone.

Hearing my sister's deliberately cheery voice made my heart hurt, suddenly and unexpectedly. My hand went up to my throat. I couldn't speak.

'Mica?' Mango said.

'Mmmmm hmmm?' I took deep breaths as my eyes welled with tears.

She heard it in my voice. 'Hey! Who cares what other people say?' my sister's voice became stern. 'I don't.'

My tears were rolling down. I still couldn't speak. Holding the phone to my ear, I brushed the falling tears away. My eyes hurt. My heart hurt.

'Mica,' Mango's voice remained stern, 'you just get yourself on that plane tomorrow. I'm going to pick you up at the airport and don't you worry about what Delilah says. She can't bloody talk, her own son is that way.'

She still couldn't say it.

Mango continued, 'Okay?'

I nodded at the phone.

'Okay?' repeated Mango.

'Okay,' I whispered.

She waited for me to say something else. I could hear her breathing.

Tears continued to pour out down my face. I whispered, 'I can't talk.'

She heard my pain, and I heard her sweet heart hurt.

I started to sob.

Mango shouted down the phone. 'Go and have a nice cup of coffee, and get your bags packed! I'll see you tomorrow at the airport! I'm coming to get you! Okay? Love you, see you tomorrow!' She hung up.

I breathed in and out, like women do when they're having labour contractions. As I sat up, the tears rolled down the front of my pyjamas, wetting my little cartoon mouse. I rubbed my face up and down harshly, pushing away the tears. My bandaids fell off my fingers and I flicked them away.

The stress of the move to Australia, studying whilst

working to pay the rent, and having the one thing that I didn't want to happen, happen, overtook my emotions. I got up and threw myself on my bed, face first. I wanted my mother, but she was dead. I cried and cried into the pillow. I thought of what she would say.

"You are a lesbian? No, no, no, no. We will see about that, but... Dirty Delilah! The sneaky way she did that. Ah, no, no, no!"

I half-smiled through my tears as I pictured her. I made her give me an imaginary hug, and I hugged her as tightly as I could in return. It wasn't enough. Laying on my bed, I rolled over and reached up to the heavens, both hands in the air, as I had many times before, stretching with all my might to reach her. I breathed deeply, trying to hold back my tears as no-one reached back to me. I shook my head in frustration, letting my hands fall back down, and thumped the mattress. I breathed long labour breaths in and out, over and over, and I let the tears roll.

On my window sill was a framed photograph of me with my father. I was about seven years old in the photo. We were standing in his yard, next to my tree. I wore a little red-checkered dress. It was terribly short. I wore white sandals on my feet, they had a slight heel to them. I remember I loved that outfit. My dad's arm hung protectively around my shoulders. Looking at that photo, I cried even more. My father had passed away earlier than my mother. I'd had a bit more time to come to terms. I was grateful I didn't have to have the "I'm gay, but not really," conversation with him. I don't think he, with his, "men should be men and women should be women" attitude, would have understood. But who knows? Who was I to assume anything, anymore?

I lay with my arms outspread, my heavy body sinking deep into the mattress, and sighed. My suitcase sat in the corner. It was time to face the music.

Chapter 14

'Ladies and Gentlemen, welcome to Brisbane. The local time is two-thirty, and the temperature is thirty-five degrees.'

There was an advertising slogan when I was growing up, which said, "Queensland, beautiful one day, perfect the next."

It was true. I looked out the window to the perfect blue skies and let the perfect sun warm my face.

With the No Seatbelt sign off, impatient passengers started to move, grabbing stuffed bags from the overhead lockers and standing prematurely in the aisles. I stayed seated and let the sun into my life for a few minutes longer.

In the terminal, I saw her waiting for me. She stood patiently on her own, her long hair neatly plaited at the back, and her hands folded in front. Her anxious eyes saw me and immediately transmitted waves of love. I smiled weakly. Her eyes suddenly welled.

I ran and hugged Mango. 'I'm okay, Mango. Really, I am okay now. Don't cry.'

We sat opposite each other in the airport coffee shop, looking out to the parked planes. Airport workers walked across the tarmac. They looked like miniature dolls walking around giant planes. I looked back to my coffee, stirring sugar in and feeling relieved that I had cried so much the day earlier. Today I felt empty but strangely fortified.

I decided to say it like it was. I sat up straight. 'I did have a relationship with a girl. Her name is Dot, but it was ages ago when I was overseas, and it wasn't serious, and I'm not gay. Who knew, she'd end up working with Dirty Delilah?' I looked down at the planes. 'I can't believe Dot told her.'

Mango said, 'She did that to hurt you.'

'Dot?'

'Yes. She did that deliberately.'

I shrugged, more concerned at the nature of how Delilah latched onto the information. I sighed. 'Fucking Delilah.'

Mango said, 'Yeah. She's going to be there tonight. With all that side of the family. You know what they're like.'

'Bring it on!' I slammed the table with such force that I startled Mango. Then I gave her such a cheeky grin that she giggled into her cappuccino. Watching her giggle made me laugh, and our tension flew away, like the planes outside, high into the air above us.

My brother and my nephews weren't going to be at the party, but my nieces, in their twenties, would be.

'Have you told the girls?' I asked.

'Mica, I have said nothing,' Mango said, forcefully.

I licked the foam from my spoon. 'Should I tell them?'

'Nope.'

'Should I tell Aunt Paloma?'

I love my Aunt Paloma, even though she is a bit too

devoted to her Jesus Cristo.

'Nope.'

'Okay.'

With caffeine in our bloodstreams and love and support in our defiant hearts, we strode to the exit.

Outside, the humidity hit me like a freight train.

I stopped in my tracks. 'God, it's hot!' I fanned my face.

'Welcome to sunny Brissy!' said my sister.

Back at Mango's place, Andrew was standing in the front reception room, a cup of tea in one hand and a jam sandwich in the other. He wore shorts. The man didn't believe in shoes or shirts. There was not an inch of fat on his scrawny, tanned body. I went to give him a kiss hello.

Andrew went straight for it. 'Are you gay?'

My sister yelled from the corridor. 'She's not gay!'

My brother-in-law shrugged. 'I don't care. It doesn't bother me!' he shouted to my sister. He looked back to me, 'Are you?'

'She's not gay!' yelled my sister again.

'Have you kissed a girl?' he asked me.

I nodded.

'She's gay!' he yelled at my sister.

Mango came back in the room. 'Go and get the back yard ready, please. You're pissing me off!'

Nothing had changed, same old, same old. Andrew was still deaf in one ear, and my sister was still yelling. I went and put my suitcase in the spare room. Sweat trickled down my back. I flapped my dress trying to let air in, and I fanned my neck with my boarding pass.

'Aunty Mica?' I heard my older niece yell. Another yeller.

I ran out to see my two grown nieces in the back lounge room. They stood with their arms outstretched. The last time I had seen them in person, they were in their late teens, with pimples, hoop earrings, and messy hair. Now they were in their twenties and had long straightened hair, expert make-up, and designer t-shirts. I looked at their lovely faces, marvelling at how adult they were. We squeezed each other in a prolonged group hug. 'Dad says you're gay!' exclaimed the older one. She'd inherited her father's social skills.

'Andrew! I told you not to say anything!' yelled my sister to the back yard.

Andrew was tossing the dog's squeaky ball. 'Huh?'

My sister moved closer to the back door and yelled louder. 'I said, I told you not to say anything!' She frowned at Andrew and nodded exaggeratedly in my direction.

'I didn't say nothing!' he yelled.

'Bullshit!' yelled my sister. 'And stop playing with the dog and get the yard ready. They'll be here soon!'

'I'm not playing with the dog!' he yelled. 'I'm cleaning!'

I rubbed my forehead. 'I've got some paracetamol

somewhere,' I said to no-one in particular. I looked at my nieces, realising they were still waiting for an answer.

'Oh, I had a girl fling, a long time ago.'

'Oh.' They nodded in unison.

'Why?' said the older niece, looking at me dumbfounded.

'Shut up! It's none of our business,' said Dolly, nudging her sister.

'I'd like to know why,' insisted the older sister, 'if you're not gay, why would you have a gay fling?'

For someone who started life without speaking, she was doing okay now. When she was a baby, Cucumber, my nickname for her, didn't speak for ages. After Cucumber's first birthday, when she still wasn't speaking, my mother exploded.

'What's wrong with her?' Mum demanded.

'Nothing's wrong with her,' we said.

'Get the scissors!' My mother abruptly stood and went looking for scissors.

My sister and I had looked confused.

'We'll cut her tongue,' said my mother, 'that will get her talking.'

My sister and I hotfooted it around the house, hiding every pair of scissors we found. Thankfully within the month, Cucumber learnt to talk, and she's never shut up since.

'Why, Aunty Mica? Doesn't that mean you're gay?' my grown niece continued.

'I don't know why, Cucumber, I just did.'

'It's none of our business,' said Dolly, frowning at her sister. 'Just leave it.'

'I don't get it. How can you just have a fling with a girl, and not be gay? Or bi?' said Cucumber. Her mind was trying to fit the pieces together. She was clearly having problems coming to terms with me kissing a woman and denying the gay sexual orientation.

'I'm not gay or bi, okay?' I said with a big sigh.

Cucumber sighed even more heavily than I did, and waved her hands in the air. 'If you say so!'

'Congratulations on your university degree!' said Dolly.

At least one of them had some tact.

'Thank you!' I smiled at her.

Dolly was the most responsible one in the family, even though she was the youngest. She was also the richest of the family, she was the only one who knew how to save. She had taught herself from a young age. Growing up with three older siblings, Dolly soon figured out if you didn't put away a little something for yourself, you would be left with nothing.

'Look at her,' Mango had said to me many years earlier.

I watched seven-year-old Dolly carry a box out the front door.

'What's in the box?'

'Food,' said Mango.

'Where's she taking it?' I said.

'Next door to Val's place.'

When Mango came back with the family shopping every Friday, Dolly took a box and filled it with one of everything, including her favourite strawberry yoghurt, and took it over to Val's house, next door. Val was a seventy-year-old widow, and she had a shelf in her fridge for Dolly's food, and a little place in her cupboard too. On Monday afternoons when Dolly's three siblings were running around the house screaming, 'There's no more cereal left! There's no more orange juice left! Where have all the biscuits gone?', Dolly was pottering over to Val's, to help herself to her cereal, bread, biscuits, popper juice, and yoghurt.

I put my arm around my responsible niece. 'Got any photos of the last few years?'

'I've got some taken not so long ago. I'll get them,' said Dolly, her face lighting up.

My nieces and I squished up on one of the old sofas in Mango's enormous lounge room, overlooking the back yard where Andrew was clearing up. Mango has plants in every corner of her lounge room, as well as hanging from the ceiling, and she has framed family photos lining the walls. An artist's charcoal caricature of my sister sits on top of the television. Mango's eyes crinkle up in the drawing.

The first photo in the album was of the girls, standing with their friend outside a modern church. Behind them to the left was an older couple. The man was standing, his arm loosely hanging around a woman's shoulders.

I gasped. 'Cameron?'

Dolly said, 'Do you know Cameron? And his wife, Annette?'

'I thought he was dead!' I said, staring closely at the photo.

Mango walked past, picking up her handbag. She shouted, 'Cameron's not dead! He's married! With twin boys!'

She disappeared back down the corridor. I stared back at the photo, smiling as I remembered the muscular arm.

Pointing to her friend in the photo, Cucumber said, 'That's our school friend, Alice. You remember her? She's gay now too.'

Dolly rolled her eyes. 'Oh my Godfather.'

I smacked Cucumber on the head. Then we went through the rest of the photographs, my nieces updating me with stories of the people in them.

A little later, while we were still sitting on the sofa, my sister raced past, to the back door.

Mango yelled to Andrew. 'I'm going to the hairdressers, and while I'm gone, you take a shower!'

Andrew was unfolding garden chairs. 'Eh?' He put his

finger up to his ear.

'Take a shower!'

Andrew sniffed himself. 'What for?'

'What for?' yelled my sister. 'It's your birthday party, that's what for!'

'I had a shower this morning!' yelled Andrew.

'Take a bloody shower!' screamed my sister as she grabbed the car keys and ran out.

In the late afternoon, as a final touch, I sprayed on Chanel N°5. I needed the big guns this evening. I stood in front of the mirror and studied myself. I wore my favourite jeans, a sleeveless flowy white V top, and my strappy heels. My hair swung down around my shoulders. I applied lots of black mascara to my lashes and put on my Dior Red Berry lipstick. Between the clothes, the make-up, the diamonte earrings, and my natural curvy body, the overall look hollered, "pura feminina." My final touch was my new clean bandage over my psoriasis patch on my forearm. I forced a smile at myself in the mirror.

'Be nice,' I said to myself.

I didn't have a plan of what I was going to do or say when I saw Delilah. I thought it best to play it by ear. My only objective was to not lose my cool. I didn't want to give her the satisfaction of seeing me affected. I straightened my back and shoulders.

'They're here!' Cucumber poked her head in my room. Her eyes were sparkling with mischief.

'You look nice,' I said. Cucumber's straight, long hair fell beautifully around her pretty face.

'Thanks,' she said. 'Delilah's with them.' Her eyes danced with anticipation.

'Well, let's go and say hello,' I said, calmly walking past her.

The other niece came running. Her tiny body was dressed in tight black trousers and a sheer black top. She wore patent black shoes on her delicate feet.

'They're here!' She looked at me. 'Aunty Mica, you look hot!'

'I know. Let's go.' I led them towards the front door.

My sister's front yard looks like a small jungle with leafy tropical trees growing over and around each other. Somewhere in the middle is a little pond, which rarely sees the light of day, and possibly has little fish in it.

From the balcony, I peered through the leafy trees, to the road. Two family sedan cars were parked behind each other. My cousins were climbing out of the first one. I heard Delilah.

'Be careful, there's sauce in there,' Delilah was telling her teenage son.

Cucumber pushed me down the stairs and through the jungle.

Mango was already at the cars, giving Delilah and her kids hello kisses. Mango's hair, make-up, and glittery black party dress looked lovely. It was the white house slippers on her feet that let her down. Out of the second car came the other Ds and my two religious aunts. My favourite aunt, a bit more butterball than when I had last seen her, rolled out of the car wearing a long colourful dress, thick beige stockings, and open-toed sandals. Plonk a hat on her head and shove a goat in her arms, and she would have been the picture-postcard woman from Peru.

'Are you sure you're covered up enough, Aunt Paloma?' I teased.

My aunt's face exploded with joy, and she stretched her arms to me. 'Ay! Hija!'

We hugged. I was pleased to see this woman with whom I had shared many fascinating conversations about life in El Salvador. Tears fell from her eyes. 'Ay hija mia, cuanto tiempo, cuanto tiempo sin verte!'

I rubbed her arms. 'It's hot, Tia! Why are you wearing so much?'

She held me back to study me. 'Que guapa estas!'

Aunt Voodoo stood waiting behind, wearing a tired look on her already bland face. She wore a long summer dress, a normal dress.

'Hola Tia,' I said.

She hadn't changed much. She wore her thick hair in the same short style, and appeared to be the same medium weight as before. The only difference was she wore fine-framed glasses now.

'Hola hija,' she said, giving me a kiss.

I walked over to Dirty Delilah. She was waiting for me. She had a big old false smile on her big old false face. I played the game and I took my time, looking at her from head to toe. Her hair was cut into a tidy bob and dyed a regrettable red colour to cover her greys. Her frilled blouse was buttoned up to her neck, starchily pressed and tucked in over her large breasts. She wore a pencil skirt and sturdy small-heeled black shoes with bows at the front. She wore glasses and stood really straight.

'Hola Mica,' she greeted me. Her head tilted to the side and her voice dripped with sympathy.

I smiled wryly. I could see Cucumber loitering, her eyes bright, watching my every move. I also saw Mango coming forward too.

'Hola Delilah,' I replied. 'Have you come straight from church?'

Delilah's false smile stayed firmly on her face. 'No.'

I leant forward and gave her, her adolescent kids and the other hyenas lurking behind, a kiss hello. Chanel N°5 lingered in their faces.

'Help me carry these!' said Mango, shoving an enormous bowl of hot tomales in my hands. Her tone may as well have said, "Don't start anything!"

I followed white slippers up the stairs and through the jungle. I felt the pack's eyes bore into the back of me, so I slowed down, climbing the stairs with deliberate steps, swaying my big ass in my tight jeans as I went.

Chapter 15

Andrew had done a good job transforming the back yard. Coloured lightbulbs hung from the eucalyptus trees and pretty fairy lights hung along the vines on the fence. The makeshift long tables had plain white paper tablecloths on them, with bows on the sides. A bunch of flowers, from the front yard jungle, sat in the middle as the centrepiece. Mango's platters of fresh prawns, crab, mussels, and oysters, lay alongside the lemons and seafood sauces. On the other table sat two enormous bowls of alfoil-wrapped hot tamales, plus plates of pupusas. Next to them were the usual salads; the Russian, the Potato, and the Rice.

Further back in the yard, Andrew's brother-in-law, Mark, a big man with messy curly blond hair, was drinking a can of beer and adjusting the pig on the spit. The smell of pork was slowly starting to fill the back yard, and the back yard itself started to fill with the arrival of more people. I hadn't seen many of the faces for years. 'Oh my God, Mica, I didn't realise you would be here! You're back from France!' was the repeated phrase as kisses and hugs were given. Their arrivals were enough to take my immediate attention away from the hyenas.

Dirty Delilah was standing by the tamales, placing serviettes and plastic forks down on the table. I watched her from across the yard.

"You might be pleasantly surprised," said Number One. "She might not say anything at all."

"Yeah, right," drawled Number Two.

Andrew walked over to me. He had showered as ordered, and was wearing jeans, and a blue and white striped shirt. I looked down at his feet. He was wearing shoes and socks.

Andrew said in his loud voice, 'Madonna's gay, you know.'

I looked around to see who had heard. Luckily there were lots of people talking, plus loud background music. Dolly was in charge of the music in the lounge room, and Beyonce's voice was blaring out. Teenagers were in the lounge, trying to out-dance each other.

'Madonna? The pop star?' I said to Andrew, my face dead-pan.

'Yeah, they say, she likes girls.'

I stared at his stupid face. He was being serious. I knew he was, I've known him a long time.

'Okay. Next time I see Madonna, the pop star, I'll ask her out. I'm going to get a tamale. Want one?'

Andrew tilted his head and put his finger behind his ear.

'Tamale!' I shouted, 'I'm getting one! Do you want one!?'

Andrew shook his head, and I walked away.

Tomales are my favourite. They are long cylindrical dumplings with meat inside. Very simple and tasty. Dirty Delilah was standing by the table. Her hyena sisters stood by the fairy lights with the hyena mother.

'Tamale, Mica?' Dirty Delilah saw me looking at the bowl.

I nodded.

'Beef or chicken?'

'Chicken.'

She handed me one of the hot alfoil cylinders. 'You like birds,' she said.

Years earlier, when I worked at Bondi Beach, my Russian manager had taught me how to say, "Thank You," to the customers, whilst really saying, "Fuck You." Basically, you say, "Thank you," but in your head, you say, "Fuck You."

'Fuck you,' I said cheerfully, taking the tamale with a smile. The intonation was spot on.

Dirty Delilah's smile remained plastered on her slightly shocked face. I walked away.

Cucumber came scuttling after me. She lowered her voice. 'Aunty Mica, you just said, "fuck you."'

I winked at Cucumber and took a bite of my hot bird tamale. Delicious.

'The pig!' Mango, who had put her dress shoes on, shouted across to Andrew, over the music.

Dolly had changed genres and had put on Andrew's favourite rock and roll songs. 'Great Balls of Fire' was playing.

'What?' said Andrew, holding a sausage roll to his mouth.

'The pig!' My sister pointed at the cooking animal. 'It's going to burn!' she shouted.

In awe, I watched Andrew shove the sausage roll, whole,

down his throat. It was like watching a boa constrictor swallow a chicken. I saw the sausage roll lump move from the top of his neck and down.

Andrew called to his brother-in-law. 'Help me turn the pig!' He tried to shout but there was the problem of a whole sausage roll getting in the way.

Mark got the message. 'Righto. I'll just get us some beers. Hang on.'

Together Andrew and Mark turned the pig around. The smell of cooking pork wafted more and more through the yard and guests kept looking to the spit, with hungry eyes.

'Not yet!' shouted Andrew to everyone, 'Er... another hour and she'll be good, I reckon!'

I took a seat next to Aunt Paloma on a bench. We watched the pig on the spit and the two jokers turning it. The light from the fire lit the yard, along with the lights Andrew had hung earlier.

Looking at my short, plump, overdressed aunt, I wondered if she would broach my personal life. Surely Aunt Voodoo had told her.

Aunt Paloma was more interested in the exotic. 'Es verdad que commen los croissants en Francia?'

'Yes, but not every day, otherwise they would be very fat.'

'Y tu vivias en la playa?'

I nodded and described Nice Beach. I told her about the Dream Team, the Desert Rats, and the Cooler Man.

'Eeee-eeee-eeee-ooooo-eeee-uuuuuup!'

She laughed at my imitation. 'Otra vez.'

With my hands cupping my mouth, I called, 'Eeee-eeee-eeee-ooooo-eeee-uuuuuup!'

She laughed and slapped her thick, brown-stockinged leg. 'Cuenta me mas,' she said.

I told her about the dodgy landlord and how he wanted me to cook him steak and vegetables each night. My aunt nodded her head and told me a story about her landlord in El Salvador. Her landlord was her elderly husband's father, Don Gonzalo. It was my aunt's job to look after her father-in-law, as his wife had died. He lived with them. Aunt Paloma told me how she had to serve him breakfast, lunch, and dinner. I shook my head in disbelief.

'Breakfast?' I said. 'Even breakfast he couldn't make for himself?'

Apparently, he couldn't. His job was to arrive at the table, and it was my aunt's job to prepare and serve.

I was outraged. 'How hard it is to make your own breakfast?' I asked. 'Bit of Cornflakes, bit of milk?'

'Nada de Cornflakes,' my aunt waved my comment away.

My aunt cooked eggs every day, in a tomato sauce. The eggs were collected from the hen pen each morning. She served breakfast with coffee and milk. The milk was fresh from the local farmer. He came each morning to my aunt's house, carrying a stainless steel cylinder. My aunt would meet him at the door, with her own container, and the farmer would pour the milk, still warm from the cow, into her container, making sure she got some of the cream too. I listened, fascinated. The elderly father-in-law would take a walk after breakfast. Aunt Paloma explained this was the time she had to clean Don Gonzalo's bedroom. She made his bed, swept the floor, and emptied his bedpan.

'His bedpan?' I gasped.

'Si,' said Aunt Paloma, matter-of-factly.

'As in, his night-time potty?' I visualised a pot filled to the brim with dark yellow urine.

'Si,' said my aunt, not understanding the horrified look on my face.

'Why didn't he just go to the toilet in the night?' I said, my voice rising in anger.

'Por que era noche,' she said, her voice calm and soft.

'I know it was night, but if you want to go to the toilet, you get up and go to the toilet!' I said.

My aunt looked at my angered face in confusion.

I continued with my rant. 'Oh my God, it's not enough that you had to make him breakfast every day, you had to empty his potty each morning too?'

My aunt frowned and clasped her hands together, not knowing what to say.

I continued. 'Did Don Gonzalo have hands?'

'Si.'

'Well?' I asked.

Aunt Paloma looked at me, shaking her confused head.

'What? He couldn't pick up his own pee and empty it himself?'

'Ah! Hija, por favor,' said my aunt. 'Era viejo, necessitaba ayuda.'

'Yeah well, when I'm old, I will be taking care of business on my own. And where was your husband, why couldn't he do it?' I asked the question, knowing it was a ridiculous one.

'Hija,' my aunt said, in a voice designed to calm me down. 'Al trabajo.'

I regretted telling my aunt about the dodgy landlord and how he asked me to cook for him. Before I could change the subject, it was changed for me. My Aunt's face froze and her eyes bulged as she stared at the ground.

'What's wrong?'

'No te muevas.'

'Why?' I froze.

She stared at my feet. I looked down.

Crawling from my empty tamales plate onto my feet, was a big gangly spider.

'Aaaaaaaaaaaaaaaaaaaaaaaaagggggggggggghhhh!' I flicked my leg, and the spider flew into the air, towards Aunt Paloma.

'Eeeeeeeeeeeeeeeeeeeeeeeeeeee!' she screamed, standing up, flapping her Peru dress.

'Oooooooh! Shit!' I said, looking around for something to flap her dress with.

She danced around and around in a circle, jigging up and down. 'Quitalo! Quitalo hija!'

I bunched up pieces of her coloured dress and flapped them around, as my aunt turned herself around and around. As she turned, I flicked, flapped, and swatted. Finally, after patting her all over, I assured my aunt the spider had gone.

My aunt took her seat on the bench. Her face was thunderous. 'Hijo de puta mierda araña!'

For such a religious woman, she certainly expressed herself colourfully.

The skinny kid from across the road came running through the back yard, looking for my sister. I watched from the bench as the boy's hands waved up and down whilst speaking to Mango and Andrew.

My sister looked around and her worried eyes found me.

'Come!' she yelled.

I followed the kid, my sister, and brother-in-law across the road. I knew the kid was the grandson of the older couple, my sister's neighbours. The older woman hated my sister. All the years they'd lived opposite, she had ignored Mango, never once a smile or a kind word. The husband was always sweet, though.

We ran into the house to see the old woman in the front room, dressed in her flannel nightdress, sitting in an old leather armchair and kicking her legs wildly. The old man was holding her down.

'Get off me, you fucking bastard!' screamed the lady.

My eyebrows went up. Ooooh la la!

'Get off me! You fucking bastard!' she screamed again.

The husband continued to fight to control his wife. There was real strength to the old woman. Her thin legs were kicking so hard she was bound to hurt herself. Andrew raced around the other side of her armchair, to try to hold her legs down. Seeing Andrew only infuriated the woman even more. Her green eyes grew larger as she spat her words to Andrew.

'Cheater! Cheater!' she hissed.

My eyebrows went up again.

My sister stood just out of reach from the woman's kicking legs. She shouted, 'Elsa? Elsa? It's me!'

Upon hearing my sister's voice, the old woman stopped moving. Her body calmed. Her face lit up with a smile. I watched, fascinated.

My sister continued in a loud voice. 'That's Andrew, Elsa! That's not who you think it is, that's Andrew!'

Andrew had relaxed his grip on the old lady's leg and moved his hand to her arm. He was too distracted looking at my sister to see it coming. Elsa bit hard on Andrew's hand.

'Aaaaagh! My fucking hand! Let go!' Andrew shouted, trying to pull his hand away. Elsa wouldn't let go.

Elsa's husband became distraught, his eyes filled with

tears.

Andrew, still trying to prise the old woman's mouth open, shouted, 'Let go, you fucking loony!'

My sister, in an authoritative tone, said, 'Elsa look at me! Elsa! It's me.'

Hearing Mango's voice again, Elsa let go of her bite and smiled lovingly at Mango. I shook my head in disbelief.

The grandson and I were still standing by the front door, frozen. I looked at the young boy. His eyes were glued to his grandmother and his little face was pale.

'Come into the kitchen,' I said, taking his arm. 'Let's make a cup of tea for your grandma.'

I learnt later that Elsa had developed dementia and went through lapses where she was convinced her husband had cheated on her. If another male approached, she got confused and thought he was her cheating husband. My sister must have resembled her own sister, whom she'd lost to a sickness many years earlier, and whom she'd loved very much. Every time she saw Mango, when she was in one of her phases, she'd smile and become girl-like. When she wasn't in one of her phases, she'd ignore Mango, as she had always done.

Back across the road, in the back yard, the air smelt of pork.

'Mmmmmmm,' I sniffed appreciatively, walking towards Aunt Paloma.

'Oh my Gawd! Mica!' A familiar voice called.

I turned to see Maria-Louisa's chubby smiling face. Her perfect teeth grinned.

'Bonjour!' I gave her a hug.

'You came!' said Mango, giving Maria-Louisa a kiss.

'Yes, can't stay long though. Robert's in the hospital,' said Maria-Louisa.

She waved her left hand at me. She wore a gold band on her fourth finger.

'Married? That's fast work!' I said.

'Not really,' laughed Maria-Louisa. 'He's a guy I'd met in London ages ago, he's Australian too, and he wasn't serious about me, until after I left to come home. After France!' She punched me on the arm. 'Oh my Gawd, how is ya friend?' she said.

Mango looked at me.

'She's fine, I think. I don't keep in contact with her.'

Maria-Louisa nodded. 'Yeah, it's like that when ya travelling. Sometimes ya really good friends with someone on ya trips, but in real life ya don't have that much in common. It happens. Oh my Gawd, that pig smells bloody good!' She gave me a playful nudge. 'Bet ya didn't get that in France! Bet ya really happy to be home now, hey!' Before I could say, 'Er, well actually,' Maria-Louisa said, 'Righto, I've gotta run. Robert's in hospital visiting his brother. Did I tell ya? He and his brother run an emu farm. Anyway, his brother had an accident chasing a bloody emu and Robert's checking on him, to see how he's recovering. I have to go and pick him up. I just wanted to pop in and wish Andrew a happy birthday, and to see ya!' Maria-Louisa hugged me tightly. 'Oh my Gawd, each time I think of those croissants on ya balcony!'

'Yes, I know! Oh, It's been really good to see you,' I said, giving her a kiss goodbye. 'Say hi to Kerrie for me.'

Mango walked Maria-Louisa to the front.

I turned to get back to Aunt Paloma. The hyenas stood metres away. I shot Dirty Delilah a false smile as I took a seat next to Aunt Paloma, who had been joined by Aunt Voodoo.

Andrew raced past us. It looked like the pig might be ready. Everyone gathered to watch Mark and Andrew hoist the pig off the spit and take it to be cut and served.

My aunts were reminiscing about their neighbour back in El Salvador, who had three children, but the youngest had one died.

'What happened to her baby? How did he die?' I asked.

My aunts gave each other a look. I recognised the look and braced myself for something ridiculous.

'He died,' said Aunt Paloma, shaking her head in great sadness.

I waited for the how.

'Malo Ojo,' said Aunt Voodoo.

'Pardon?'

'Malo Ojo,' she repeated. Her face was weary.

This is where my level of anger shoots from zero to one hundred, in about a second.

'The child died from the Evil Eye?' I asked, my voice shrill.

My aunts nodded their heads. 'Si.'

My brain was on the verge of combustion. 'The child was a perfectly healthy baby?'

They nodded.

'And one day he died, just died suddenly?'

They nodded.

'Because someone in the village gave him the Evil Eye?'

They nodded.

I scratched at the bandage on my arm. My blood was boiling, not at the story, but at their firm belief of the story. I could not comprehend their having no desire to even suggest another alternative, like, I don't know, "He had a very high temperature and they didn't have any medicine." For my aunts, it was irrefutably the Evil Eye. I should have walked away at this stage.

'Why would someone give an innocent baby the Evil Eye?'

My aunts sighed.

Aust Paloma said in a soft tone, 'Era celosa.'

'Who was jealous?' I shook my head, not understanding a damn thing. 'Of?'

Apparently, the woman who put the Evil Eye on the baby was in love with the baby's father. I nodded, taking it all in. I thought I might verbalise it, just to make sure I got it correct.

'She was in love with the lady's partner, the father of the baby, so she put Evil Eye on the baby, to hurt the lady?'

'Si!' My aunts nodded, happy that I was finally understanding.

'And not Evil Eye on the mother's other two children?' I asked.

'Other two children, different father,' said Aunt Voodoo.

'Of course,' I said, standing up, looking at the party guests queueing for the pork. 'I'm going to go and get a drink now. Goodbye,' I said.

I walked away finishing that sentence in my head, "... you freaks!" Who believes this stuff? I realised that no matter how much logic I threw at my aunts, they would remain firm in their beliefs.

I had a sudden insight. I turned back. 'You had to go to Church every week when you were young?' I asked.

'Every week,' they nodded, 'we all went. Except your mother.'

I smiled. 'Because?'

'She stopped going after her first boyfriend died. She said God refused to help him.'

I couldn't help myself. 'And how did he die?'

'Poisoning.'

'Food poisoning, in a restaurant?' I was horrified to think of a young fifteen or sixteen-year-old in this situation.

They shook their heads. I waited for it.

'The Orange Tree.'

I waited for more.

'He loved oranges,' my Aunt Paloma took over the story, 'and everyone knew that. So they poisoned the oranges on the orange tree.'

I said, 'Probably they were jealous he was dating my mother.'

My aunts nodded matter-of-factly.

Aunt Paloma said a little prayer. 'Señor, cuida Josalito, cuidalo bien.'

I took a deep breath and I continued my line of enquiry. 'In church, in El Salvador, does God think that sex is only for married couples?'

I stared at the ground, not sure why I said the obvious. My Aunts nodded.

'But I've heard lots of stories about women having babies from different fathers, and they aren't all married.'

'Ay hija,' they said, giving me a resigned look.

What did that mean? No idea. I continued.

'What about gay people? What does Jesus say about gay

people?'

Number One suddenly woke up. "Why bring up gay people?"

Number Two woke up too. "Yeah, why did you bring it up? You weren't even talking about gay people! And now you've gone and brought it up."

Aunt Paloma smiled. I thought this was a good sign.

'We pray for gay people. It's not natural.'

My face dropped and I took a huge step back.

'But Evil Eye and orange poisoning is?!'

Looking at my Aunt's elderly faces, I saw lines of true hardship etched into them. They'd lived severe lives, and they'd remained sane by holding onto their religious and witchcraft beliefs. The heat of my boiling blood cooled a little. I tried to breathe acceptance.

'Okay. Okay, ' I said, shrugging my resigned shoulders. 'I'm going to get a drink.'

'Hija?' said Aunt Voodoo.

'Yes?' I turned back to look at her hard face.

'Gay people need help. We are all praying for them to become normal,' she said, looking into my eyes with sadness.

Aunt Paloma sat next to her, not looking at me. She sat, bowing her head and folding her hands, as if in prayer. The left-over fire from the pig on the spit flickered. I pictured myself roasting on that very spit, with the hyenas and my

Aunt Paloma standing by, reciting prayers. Looking at my aunts, sitting there with worry in their souls, I realised I would not be able to undo years of beliefs. What I could do is, not give them any of my energy or time, regarding this subject.

I smiled brightly and once again said, 'I'm going for a drink." I pointed to the spit, "You should get some pork.'

'Hija?' Aunt Paloma lifted her head.

'Yes?'

'If you want, you can come to our house,' she said.

'So we can pray for you,' said Aunt Voodoo. 'Tonight, if you like, after the party.'

The fire from the spit flared up as someone threw a piece of fat on it. My body took in the heat and the insulting inference from my aunt's words. Out of the corner of my eye, I could see the hyenas hovering to the side. I felt them watching, waiting, for my reaction. I scratched my bandage. I shook my head in disgust and disbelief that those words had just come out. I walked away.

Number Two wasn't disgusted, just amused. "You brought it up, Loser! And now they want to whisk you away to their house, put you in the back yard under the moon, and do the spell stuff! Jesus Christ!"

Number One agreed. "Jesus, Joseph, Mary! Please give me patience."

I marched past Dolly with her music in the lounge room. She saw my rigid body.

'Aunty Mica, are you okay?' she said, as I stomped past.

'Yes!'

'I saved you a plate of pork!' she called after me. 'It's in the kitchen cupboard, bottom shelf behind the potatoes!'

I stormed down the long corridor, to the kitchen. It was empty. I leant back against the bench, scratching my bandage and taking deep labour breaths. I looked around. The kitchen looked how my mind felt; it was chaotic, not a spare inch of space. Dirty plates stacked up in wonky piles amongst empty wine bottles and empty packets of crisps. The sink was full of glasses and cutlery.

I went to the pantry and opened it. It smelt of pork. I looked on the bottom shelf. There it was, where she said it would be, behind the potatoes and next to a bottle of scotch. I found a clean glass and I poured myself a very large scotch. I flung the freezer door open and pulled out the ice tray and bang-bang-banged it. I could hear Aunt Voodoo's voice saying, "So we can pray together, for you." I smashed the ice tray against the sink once more and got the cubes out and into my glass. With shaky hands, I lifted the scotch to my lips.

"At least Dirty Delilah hasn't said anything," said Number One.

"Wait for it," said Number Two.

Chapter 16

'We have to do it now, Andrew!' yelled Mango, running into the kitchen. Her black eyes glared with anger.

Andrew came running. 'Yeah, he's just clearing a space,' he said.

I stood in the corner, watching. Mango yanked open the drawer, pushing aside spoons, knives, forks, bottle-openers, spatulas, and potato peelers.

'I need the big ones,' she said, foraging.

She pulled out two big knives and shoved one in my hand.

'Have you got the lighter?' she shouted to Andrew.

Andrew patted his shirt pocket. 'Yeah.'

'Well, hurry up. Jules needs to get Uncle Lindsey home to have his medicine!' she yelled.

'Okay!' Andrew yelled back.

'Don't yell at me!' shouted Mango. Her face screwed up, all crinkly.

'You're yelling at me!' shouted Andrew, looking hurt.

'Because you won't help me with the bloody cakes!'

'I'm here, aren't I?!'

My sister grabbed my arm by my psoriasis bandage.

'Come on, Mica, let's cut these bloody cakes. It's his

birthday and he won't even help me.'

In the lounge room, Dolly was putting the candles in her father's cake.

Andrew pointed with a smile. 'It's a limousine!'

Mango shoved the cake in his hands. 'Take the bloody thing outside!'

'Wait!' said Dolly. 'Where's the lighter?'

'Here,' said Andrew, nodding to his pocket.

Dolly lit the five and the zero candles. 'Go, Dad!'

Andrew started.

'Wait!' yelled Mango. 'Light this one,' she told Dolly.

Mango shoved my cake into my hands. It was a large white rectangular cake, decorated with strawberries and it had red fancy writing on it, "Congratulations Mica!" It smelt exactly how I did the week after I finished highschool, like rum. Dolly lit the thick candle and it erupted into sparkles inches from my face.

'Bloody hell!' I said, holding the cake at arm's distance.

Andrew and I moved with our cakes, and the guests came towards us.

'Happy Birthday to you, Happy Birthday to you, Happy Birthday, Dear Andrew, Happy Birthday to you! … and congratulations, Mica!'

Everyone applauded as Andrew and I reached the long wooden tables and set the cakes down. Family and friends gathered and shouted, 'Hip Hip Hooray!'

Andrew blew his candles out, then said, 'Blow yours out.'

My big candle spattered out sparkling flames. There was no way I was going to be able to blow it out. I shook my head.

'Blow it out,' repeated Andrew.

Mango came, with her knife in her hand. 'No, Andrew!' she shouted, 'It just fizzles out on its own!' Three seconds later, it did. It fizzled out and everyone applauded.

'Congratulations, Mica!'

'Thank you!' I said, giving Mango a huge kiss on the cheek. 'Thank you, Mango.'

Cucumber came forward with a camera. 'We didn't get the photos. Light it again for the photo.'

Mark leant forward and lit Andrew's five and zero.

'Wait!' said Dolly running forward, holding her cousin's one-year-old baby in her arms. 'Get a photo with Timmy in it too!' She positioned herself next to her father and smiled, ready for the camera.

'Watch that baby!' yelled my sister.

Too late, the baby had reached and grabbed the candle flame. His baby face turned red and his eyes watered before letting out the almighty 'Waaaaaaaaaaaah!'

My horrified niece ran inside with the little one to cool his burning fingers.

'Again,' said Cucumber, positioning herself in front of Andrew and the cake.

Mark leant forward and relit the Five candle.

'Smile, Dad!' said Cucumber.

People starting singing, 'For he's a jolly good fellow...'

Over the singing voices, Andrew shouted to me. 'Why didn't you bring your girlfriend?'

'What?' I regretted the question, because I had heard him.

Just as everyone finished singing, 'And so say all of us', Andrew shouted. 'Why didn't you bring your girlfriend?'

Everyone heard it, loud and clear. Kids put their hands over their mouths. One said, 'Uhm mah!' The adults stood still. Cucumber was staring at me, and so were the hyenas.

My sister said in her loud voice, 'Don't listen to him, Mica!' picking up her knife and harshly cutting Andrew's cake. 'He's a bloody dickhead!' She slammed a piece of chocolate limousine cake onto a plate and shoved it into Andrew's hand. 'Happy Birthday, Andrew!' she shouted.

The back yard remained frozen, nobody moved, all eyes were on me. I froze too, staring down at the white frosting on my cake. My worst fear had now really and truly just happened. Everyone had heard and now there was total silence, except for the crackling noise from the dying spit fire, and Dolly's background music. Paul Anka was crooning out 'Diana'.

Cucumber's eyes scanned the group, looking for reactions. The Dirty D's teenage kids started whispering.

Delilah valiantly hushed them, reproaching them like the saint she was.

I heard giggles coming from the back. I also heard voices in my head. They were speaking at the same time, one on top of the other.

'You're so paranoid,' said Dot's voice.

'Always wear jeans,' said my mother's voice.

'Still trying!' said my voice.

'What's wrong with you? Why don't you ever have a boyfriend?' said my brother's voice.

'Girls who like girls.' I heard Mango's voice.

'Men should be men and women should be women,' said my father's voice.

Something deep inside clicked. A different voice, a new calm voice coming from the bottom of my gut, said, "They will think what they think. You can't control them. You are who you are, and that is enough." I took a long deep breath.

Number Two couldn't help herself. "Yeah, but, they want a show. Give them a show!"

I turned to Andrew and said loudly, 'My girlfriend is in Sydney looking after our dog, on our balcony, with our lesbian friends. She'll come to the next family party.'

Whispers raced throughout the crowd. Mango shot me the death look.

Meanwhile, Andrew, holding his limousine cake, looked

like he had finally got the response he had been searching for. His eyes danced, like his daughter's had earlier in the evening, and his smile spread wide. 'Yeah? What's she like?'

I made an hourglass figure in the air with my hands. Andrew's smile grew, and the crowd gasped.

Mango furiously cut into Andrew's limousine cake, dividing it into spare parts. I topped off my routine with a dazzling smile. I turned to face the shocked crowd and my eyes found and rested on Dirty Delilah. Her scheming eyes were on me, sparkling with pure satisfaction. Her teenage kids, standing next to her, were grinning and giggling, as were her hyena sisters. I looked over at my aunts further back in the crowd. Their catholic heads were lowered in prayer.

Dolly, who was in the lounge room with the baby on her hip, turned the music up. 'Jailhouse Rock' came blaring out.

Mango busied herself with Andrew's birthday cake.

'How long have you been gay?' shouted Delilah over the music.

People gasped.

I stared at the hyena. 'I was born gay,' I shouted, 'just like you were born vindictive.'

Mango jumped into action. 'Who wants the chocolate cake?' she shouted. 'Jules? Do you want a piece to take home? What about Uncle Lindsey? Desley? You want the chocolate cake? Laura?'

People shuffled towards Andrew's cake.

'I wasn't born vindictive!' shouted Delilah over the moving people.

'No,' I shouted, 'you were born vindictive and raised closed-minded!'

Aunt Paloma started praying, 'Ah Señor, ayudala, ayudala. Por favor.'

'I don't need any of your God's help!' I shouted to my aunts. 'I don't need help from people who believe in snakes and Evil Eye and orange tree poisoning and little pins and voodoo!' I lifted my knife high up in the air. 'Now,' I smiled brightly and changed my tone, 'who would like a piece of the girl cake?'

'She's drunk!' one of the older guests said.

Disapproving voices whispered throughout the crowd.

Delilah stepped forward, her chest sticking out defiantly. Before she could speak, Mango moved next to me and said, 'This is Mica's night, Delilah. Just drop it!'

Dirty Delilah put on her false smile and said, 'Yes. It's time to leave anyway. Thank you for the party, Mango.'

'You're welcome!' barked Mango.

Delilah turned to leave and said in a low voice for my ears only, 'At least I'm not gay.' She walked over to the hyenas and they gathered their belongings.

My niece Cucumber came forward, frowning, pushing her long hair from her face. She leant in close. 'Aunty

Mica,' she whispered, 'I thought you said...'

'Honey, I've got a knife in my hand.'

Cucumber skipped over to her mother for a piece of the limousine.

Chapter 17

Standing at the two-minute drop-off/pick-up point at Sydney Airport, I watched Casey's four-wheel-drive pull up. She leant over to open the passenger door. She was wearing jeans, a white t-shirt, and a white bandana over her blonde hair.

'Well?' she asked, maneuvering the car out of the airport.

'The bandana suits you.'

'I meant you. What happened?' she said, keeping her eyes on the road.

'I came out of the closet,' I said, stretching my hands out in front of me.

'What?' she said, turning her head to look at me. Her big blue eyes grew in size.

'They were expecting it.'

'Mica! No!' she sighed. There was a lot of disappointment and frustration in that sigh. 'Mica, you're still lying! You're going around in circles!' she said, shaking her bandana'd head.

'I know.' My tone was resigned. 'They wanted me to go to my aunt's place for a prayer session,' I said, sitting up straight.

'What?'

'To pray away the lesbian in me.'

'What?'

'I didn't, of course. Let them put their spells on me from afar.'

'Seriously! Your family!' She shook her head, trying to comprehend. 'And when they see you with a boyfriend? What are you going to do then?'

She took the next exit off the freeway.

'They'll think it was their praying.'

'Yeah, they will,' she agreed. 'But why do you have to complicate things?'

I ignored that question and looked at my short fingernails and my new bandage on my forearm. I lifted my wrist for a sniff of La Panthere.

'Does your sister at least know you're straight?' said Casey after a while.

'Yes. She is not amused.'

At the end of the party, when everyone had left, Mango and I had sat in the back room drinking cups of milky tea on the old sofa. Mango had put her white fluffy slippers on and had loosened her hairdo.

'Why did you say that?' Mango asked me, putting a piece of the strawberry rum cake in her mouth.

'It's good, isn't it?' I pointed to the cake.

She nodded begrudgingly. 'Why?'

'It just came out.'

'Because you wanted to make trouble!'

'No, I didn't.'

'Yes, you did!'

'Hey!' Andrew came into the room. He had changed into his favourite piece of clothing, his old shorts, and nothing else. 'Where's my cup of tea?'

'I asked you if you wanted one!' shouted my sister.

'Ay? Oh. I didn't hear you,' said Andrew.

'You never hear me!' yelled my sister.

I walked over and cut myself another piece of the rum cake. I looked to Mango. 'You want another?'

She nodded, and I took her plate for a refill. Best to keep her mouth busy.

Casey took the next right into the city streets, and we slowed in the traffic.

'She definitely knows you're not gay?'

'Yes. My brother-in-law is convinced I'm gay though, and Cucumber is confused.'

'And your cousin? The one who worked with Dot?'

'Dirty Delilah. She's extremely happy that I am gay,' I said.

Casey shook her head in exasperation.

The traffic got thicker as we turned to go over the Harbour Bridge. We were travelling at forty kilometres per hour. I looked down at the Opera House, and to the sparkling water.

'It's such a spacious country,' I said, noticing the few boats on the water.

'Australia?'

I nodded.

'Australia? Your country?' Casey said sarcastically.

'It doesn't feel like my country.'

'I know. You love Europe.'

'Mmmmm hmmmm.'

'Are you going to go back now you've finished uni?'

'Can't afford to straight away.'

Casey turned right into Military Road and her eyes lit up. 'Maybe you'll meet an Aussie guy, and stay,' she said.

We drove past my favourite takeaway Thai restaurant on the right.

'Maybe pigs will fly.'

'Never say never, Mica.'

Four minutes later, Casey turned into my leafy street. We slowed down just before we got to the water. Johno was out the front, looking in his letterbox. He was wearing his rugby shorts and t-shirt.

'G'day!' He waved as he saw us.

'Hello!' We called from the car.

I reached to get my bag.

'Tomorrow night?' Casey looked at me.

'Yes!' I said, smiling. 'It's going to be a fun night!'

'You bet! We really do need to properly celebrate you finishing university. It's a big deal. And celebrate you finally telling your sister about Dot. Even though you got it a bit wrong. A lot wrong. At least now, it really is all over.'

'O-V-E-R!' I spelt it out to the sky.

'You're not gay. Meet you about seven tomorrow? Balmoral Beach.' Casey said, leaning against the steering wheel.

I leant over to give her a peck on the cheek. 'Yes.' I jumped out and closed the car door. Leaning through the window, I said, 'Tomorrow night. I'm not gay.'

'You are not gay.' She repeated.

'Come what may! Touche! I like the boys in Norway!' I laughed, waving goodbye.

She drove off with a happy toot.

Balmoral Beach is the other side of Ooooorstraaaaliyah Mosman. I walked up my hilly street, crossed Military Road, and stopped to look in the shop windows. Christmas was at the end of the month, and the shops had changed their displays. I stopped in front of a bakery. Pretty green and red ribbons curled in and around a mountain of mince pies. I felt a sudden longing for Marks and Spencer on the Kings Road. I wished for a time machine, which would give me half an hour to browse the glorious dessert section of Marks and Spencers. I loved the chocolate Yuletide logs, the snowflake shortbreads, the snowbomb sponge cakes, the mince pies, the traditional Christmas cakes, and even though they weren't Christmas desserts, I totally loved the creamy trifles. I sighed.

I crossed the street and started the walk down the hill, past the houses with million-dollar water views. It took me under a half hour to walk down. Quite a few people had already gathered, and the grassy part was dotted with picnic blankets and families. I scanned the crowd till I saw Casey, Moira, and Elisa, near the white rotunda. I started weaving my way through.

'Bonsoir Ladies!' I greeted the girls.

'This was handy for you,' said Elisa, holding her hand over her eye to keep out the sun, as she looked up.

'Yeeeee-arse,' I said with a grin, kneeling beside them and spreading my picnic blanket out. 'I walked here.' I planted two kisses on the girls' cheeks.

Moira was looking as elegant as ever in a flowing summer dress and freshly washed, wispy hair. Casey looked smart-casual in jeans and a pretty silk top, the same blue colour as her eyes. Elisa had on checkered slacks and a fitted white short-sleeved shirt. I wore my trusty jeans and my Harrak ma ella top.

I dug into my bag. 'Kalamata olives, tapenade and a type of focaccia bread. It has olives in it.'

Moira gave me a generous smile. 'I sense a theme, Mica.'

'Yes!' I laughed, placing the goodies next to the girl's

picnic.

It was a beautiful day. I relaxed back on my blanket, looking up to the sky, feeling free from university, family, and secrets. I looked over at the beach.

'They have a shark sign on this beach.' I nodded to the yellow sign which read, "Enclosure NOT sharkproof."

'Yeah,' said Casey.

'It doesn't look like this beach would have sharks, it's too calm. Deceptive, huh?' I said.

'Like you,' smiled Elisa.

'Do you know what to do if you see a shark in the water, Elisa?'

'Get out?'

'If you don't have time to get out. What do you do?'

'Pray?'

'Punch him on the nose,' I said, looking at her with a dead-pan expression.

Elisa broke out a huge smile. 'I think that's quite enough of your wisdom for today. Please refrain from sharing further.'

'As you wish.' I stretched my legs out in front of me.

'Shut up and drink.' Elisa handed me a glass of champagne.

Casey did the toast. 'To Mica finishing her university!'

'To Mica finishing her university!'

The beach was quickly filling up with friends, families, picnic blankets, deck chairs, and drink coolers. We nodded hello to the people setting up in the grassy space next to us. All around were sounds of popping wine corks, beer bottle tops being twisted, and children's laughter as they ran from the beach to their parent's blanket. More and more people arrived for the Carols by Candlelight, till the beach was choc-a-block. Judging by all the polo shirts and leather sandals, I gathered these people were the people who owned the million-dollar houses just above. It was quite "Ooooorstraaaaliyah Darling".

When it came to "Ooooorstraaaaliyah Darling", my little group was included of course. Casey lived in Manly with sea views. Elisa and Moira lived in inner-city Paddington with a dog that ate organic pig ears, and I lived in Mosman, two minutes from the harbour. I was renting however, and could barely afford it, so that made me a pretend "Ooooorstraaaaliyah Darling", which is even worse.

It had been several years since I'd had a summer Christmas and I was finding the concept of Ooooorstraaaaliyah Carols by Candlelight on the beach, to be hilarious. Kids ran around the white Rotunda wearing shorts, t-shirts, and sandals. Not one of them wore boots, a scarf or a beanie. Had I forgotten that Santa and the beach belonged together? In recent years, I'd looked forward to Christmas more because of the markets with big fat German sausages, vins chauds, hot chocolates, and little kids bundled up like moonwalkers. I love Hyde Park at the best of times, but when it snows and it's Winter Wonderland time, it's magical. It gets dark so early, and the lights of the rides illuminate that corner of the park with excitement. People stroll, eating sugar-coated peanuts, rugged up in their boots, gloves, scarves, and hats.

I had never worn a scarf until I was seventeen, when I went to Spain for my exchange year, the same year I kissed lovely Javier. Wintertime had arrived and the Spanish people got out their hats, gloves, and scarves.

'Hola. Cuanto para esta bufanda, por favor?'

I bought myself a pretty pink striped scarf at the market, from the man who also sold beige bras and enormous underpants.

The next day I asked my Scottish friend, also spending a school year in Spain, 'How do you get your scarf into that knot?'

'What do you mean?' She looked at me.

'How do you make it into that knot?' I pointed to her scarf.

'Are you telling me you've never worn a scarf before?'

'I've never worn a scarf before.'

Delighted at my virginity, she gave me a demonstration of a few different ways one might want to wear a scarf.

The same Scottish friend was less delighted when one day we walked passed an old bridge, just outside of Seville. We were on a school excursion.

That morning, my Spanish host-mother had run around the kitchen like a mad woman. 'Toma, lleva esto,' she said, wrapping a football-sized bread roll, filled with freshly fried eggs and ham, in alfoil. She shoved the hot football in my hands. 'Y esto,' she said, cutting a huge chunk of sheep's cheese. She got the alfoil again. 'Y esto,' she said, giving me half a chorizo.

'Algo mas?' I asked jokingly.

'Y esto,' she said, shoving an orange in my hands.

We all took our mothers' lunches with us on the excursion to Seville, where I saw "the bridge". My uncultured eyes couldn't believe what they were seeing.

I pointed to the bridge and said to my Scottish friend, 'Look! People made that with their hands, you know. Have you ever seen anything so old?'

My Scottish friend shook her perplexed head.

A few years later, I travelled to her home town of Edinburgh, and as I stood looking from one beautiful old bridge to the next, I let the laughter rise up out of me. She could have teased me about my ignorance that day, but she never did. She must have been too stunned.

As I looked around Balmoral Beach this Christmas Carol day, there were no scarves. Some kids were wearing sun hats, even though it was past seven in the evening. Australian children must wear hats at school, during outdoor break-times, it's obligatory. The school hats I'd seen were ugly floppy hats, dangling over the poor kid's head like a giant lazy cracked egg. We didn't have that rule when I was at school. To the contrary, in my all-girls catholic school, once the lunch bell rang, we raced outside to fight over who got to sit on the hot bench in the midday sun, and we pulled our uniforms up as high as we could, to tan our legs. We had year-round tans from our knickers down to our socks.

My father chose that catholic school for me. My mother certainly didn't. Every day when I walked out the door to go to school, she'd say, 'Don't listen to those nuns. They've never lived a day in their lives.' Of course, she always added, 'And don't let the priests touch you.'

Casey poured more champagne. She lifted her glass for another toast.

'To Mica coming out to her family, even though she's not gay!'

'Hear, hear!' cheered Moira, lifting her glass. 'To her not being gay!'

My head looked left and right, checking to see if that loud comment had gotten the interest of these good Pinot-Grigio-drinking, million-dollar-view people.

Elisa lifted up her glass. 'Hear, hear!' she repeated, adding, 'to her being gay!'

'Very funny, Elisa,' I said, lifting my glass. 'How about, to my family, immediate family, not caring either way!'

'Hear, hear!' Everyone clinked glasses loudly on that one.

I took a slow sip of champagne, adoring the numbing sensation spreading through my body. I leant back, my hands on the grass, and felt something crawl over me.

'Ahhhh!' I shrieked, sending my champagne flying.

Casey laughed and picked up a leaf. 'What did you think it was?'

'Spider? Cockroach?'

'You're paranoid,' she laughed.

Elisa picked up the champagne bottle and gestured for me to lean in with my empty glass. As she poured she softly said, 'Come out of the closet!'

Laughing, I punched her on her arm and whispered, 'Shut up and pass the crisps.'

She passed me the packet. 'We call them chips,' she whispered, 'you faux wannabe European.'

I punched her on the other arm. Laughing, I looked up to see Moira, sitting poised with her long bare legs tucked under her flowing dress, watching us with surveying eyes. I slunk back on my blanket.

I relaxed into the community atmosphere. The children's excitement was helping to build the adult's excitement. Little bodies kept running around saying, 'When are we going to sing, Mummy?'

Mothers kept reassuring. 'Soon. Go and play on the swings.'

I watched the kids run and play, and suddenly felt light after a busy and emotional year.

'This is a good picnic blanket, where did you get it?' asked Casey, admiring the sturdiness of my blanket.

'Dot gave it to me.'

'How did that finish up?' asked Moira.

'I told her she made sick and I hated her,' I said.'That was a bit rude, don't you think?' said Elisa, gently.

'No.'

'And immature?' said Moira.

'No.'

'Oh, Mica!' said Casey in her frustrated tone.

'The band is coming!' I pointed to a short guy walking into the Rotunda. He was dressed in a tuxedo and carrying a violin. Saved by the violin! More tuxedos, black dresses, and instruments followed to take their places in the Rotunda.

The public gathered their children to their blankets to sing. 'Grab the song sheets, ready? Where are the words?'

The more champagne I guzzled, the more confidently I sang. The problem was, so did the people next to us. Their guy had an impressive set of lungs on him. He was a large fellow with a beer belly and he was bellowing it out. We tried to keep up but the guy was getting louder and louder.

At the end of, 'O Come Let Us Adore Him,' I looked at Mr Big Lungs unadoringly, and with exasperated judgemental eyes. He gave me a cheeky wink, and I surrendered a smile.

Pop! Moira opened another bottle just as 'Away In A Manger' started.

'Pass me your glass, Mica.'

We drank and we sang the entire evening.

Towards the end, the skies darkened and the street lamps illuminated the choir in the Rotunda. We read our lyrics by mobile phone torchlight. As the last violin string was strung, people on picnic blankets all over the beach broke into applause. Mr Big Lungs next door applauded and cheered the loudest and longest, of course. The choir accepted the appreciation, taking bows. Finally, after the applause had calmed, the cellist made the first move, standing from behind her instrument. Taking her cue, the contented and weary public started packing up too.

Casey swung her empty glass back and forth. She looked at me with cheeky blue eyes. I knew that look.

'I don't feel like going home,' she said.

Chapter 18

Casey was feeling it. She was standing tall. Her blonde hair fell around her shoulders, her silk top accentuated her breasts, and her blue jeans hugged her curves.

Back at Balmoral Beach, we had agreed it would be one of the Manly pubs we would grace with our Christmas Carol drunken presence. Designated Driver, Moira, drove us.

'Sure you won't join us?' I'd asked, when I tumbled out of the car onto Manly Esplanade.

'No, thanks. You two have fun,' said Moira. 'Go and kiss a fella!' she teased me.

Elisa added, 'Or a woman.'

Casey sauntered into the harbourside pub. I skipped behind her, in my maternity top and flat shoes.

Too drunk to remember not to mix drinks, I ordered at the bar. 'A scotch and coke, and a gin and tonic, please.'

The pub was heaving, and the music was turned up. Paul Kelly's voice sang through the speakers. Over the loud music, lots of well-dressed men talked to lots of pretty women with shiny eye make-up. I looked to my left. Casey was chatting to a man dressed in a crisp white shirt and jeans. He had dark brown hair and looked fit, like he might work outside, perhaps as a beach lifeguard.

I looked at my watch. 'Three minutes,' I murmured. 'Not bad.'

Taking our drinks, I walked over and placed them on the

little table by Casey. I gave her a nudge to let her know they were there.

I walked outside to the beer garden. There was already a queue of girls for the toilets. A couple of girls did the "I really need to do a wee" dance. I stood, trying to think of anything but running water, which was difficult because between the Ladies and the Mens, there was a long trough with four taps, and above it, a long mirror. Each time someone came out, they washed their hands. Damn it. Distract. Distract.

"Apple crumble," said Numer One. "You haven't eaten Apple Crumble in years."

"Or Custard," said Number Two.

The queue for the men's toilets on the opposite side moved much faster.

A woman in a long-flowing dress came out of a cubicle and I moved to the front of the queue with a grateful smile. The next cubicle opened and as I stood aside to let the girl pass, a cheeky young Miss Blue T-shirt pushed past and dashed into my cubicle. My drunken eyes frowned.

'That's not fair,' said a guy, standing over in the men's queue.

I gave the guy a weak smile and a shrug.

Back in the noisy bar, I spotted Casey. She was sitting with the lifesaver. I picked up my drink. Casey didn't even notice me, her blue eyes were locked on her beach man. I stood, taking a sip of my scotch and coke, looking around. After a little while, I saw him sitting by the bar. I walked over.

'You're the guy from the loo,' I said.

'I am,' he nodded, recognising me. He pointed to the free barstool. 'Would you like a seat?'

He introduced himself as Robin. Then he introduced me to a woman and man, standing by him.

'Mica, this is Avery.'

'Hello,' she said in a South African accent. We shook hands.

"How formal," said Number Two.

'And this is Dingo,' said Robin, gesturing to the scruffy-looking man next to Avery.

Dingo gave me a wave.

"How informal," said Number Two.

Robin asked if I was out for a special occasion.

'Oh come all ye faithful,' I said.

'Joyful and triumphant,' he said.

I laughed and told him about the Balmoral Christmas Carols. He told me he was a local, out for a drink after work.

Robin was about my age. He had blue eyes and short brown hair. I looked at his formal clothing. He wore a suit and glasses. His jacket was hanging on a hook under the bar.

"Totally not your type. Relax," said Number Two.

'Drink?' asked Robin.

Robin ordered drinks, including for blonde Avery and shabby Dingo, standing further along the bar.

Robin passed me my scotch. 'Are you here with someone?'

I looked around in a slight panic as Casey had completely gone out of my mind. I saw her on the other side, talking to the lifeguard. Their eyes were fixed on each other. It could only be a matter of time.

'Yes,' I said.

Robin waited for further information. I didn't give it.

'Are you?' I asked.

He nodded yes. I waited for further information. He didn't give it.

I looked at his black-rimmed glasses.

"So not your type," said Number Two. "Relax."

'Which is your favourite Christmas carol?' Robin said.

'Last Christmas.'

'Wham?'

I nodded, sipping my scotch through a straw.

'That's not a Christmas carol,' he said.

'Yes, it is.'

'No, it is not.'

'Define Christmas carol.'

'You don't know this about me, but I am a master definer.'

'Here we go,' I said, sitting up in anticipation.

"Okay, he's fun, but still not your type," said Number Two. "Relax."

Robin and I slipped into a speaking marathon and he had me laughing from the first minute. And one minute turned into one hour, which turned into three hours. All this time, Paul Kelly kept singing, the drinks kept coming, and the conversation rolled.

Robin talked fantastically fun nonsense. 'Rick Astley cannot be considered a Christmas singer,' he said.

'Yes, he can.'

'You're wrong.'

'"Never gonna give you up". What could be more Christmassy than that?' I said.

'ACDC could be considered more Christmassy,' he said. Turning to the barman, he said, 'Another round, please.'

'Highway to Hell' is a Christmas cry for redirection?'

Robin laughed. 'To the freeway to heaven.'

'He took the wrong exit?'

Robin nodded. 'Needs to do a u-turn, and take the M6 to Bethlehem.'

Avery came over and Dingo excused himself to go and have a cigarette. Avery stood between Robin and me, interrupting our important Christmas hymn discussion.

'Would you like to sit?' I asked, readying myself to stand.

Avery shook her blonde hair. 'No, I like standing, thank you.'

She was very pretty. She was tall with beautiful almond eyes, amazing cheekbones, and perfect creamy skin.

'Did I hear you say something about France before?' she said.

'Yes, I lived there, before here,' I said.

'I'm studying French at the moment!' she said, clapping her hands.

This girl was as sloshed as I was, and we had a drunken, grammatically poor discussion in French about which restaurant did the best Yum Cha in Sydney's China Town. Her beautiful eyes looked upwards every five seconds as she searched for her words in French, making her look even drunker than she already was, which made me feel drunker than I already was, which was very, very, very. It was hard enough speaking English, let alone French. My brain was relieved when Dingo came back because he and Avery went back to their chatting. Before she left though, Avery's hand lightly touched Robin's shoulder.

I clocked it, even in my drunken state. I looked into Robin's eyes. 'Is she your girlfriend?'

Taking my hand in his, under the bar, Robin nodded. 'Another drink?'

The drinks never stopped, and neither did our talking marathons. We talked over each other, under each other, in and around each other, all evening, and all the time secretly holding hands under the bar.

'I didn't think his performance was... adequate,' said Robin, continuing with his story.

'Great adjective,' I nodded, drawn into his funny storytelling.

'Mica?' I heard Casey's voice and dropped Robin's hand.

'Mica, I'm going,' Casey said, holding her bag.

I gestured from Casey to Robin. 'Robin, this is Casey, and her lifesaver friend.'

Everyone shook hands.

Casey kissed me goodbye. 'Call me tomorrow.'

'Yes, I will.'

I watched Mr White Shirt guide Casey through the bar, his hand on her back. I swung back around to face Robin.

He looked at me. 'So...,' he said slowly, 'your friend has left.'

My brown eyes looked to his. 'Yes.'

'What happens now?' he asked, taking my hand underneath the bar.

"Well, that's a damn fine question, Brother, cause we had a blackout, didn't we!?" said Number Two, the next day.

I woke up and the wooden-beamed ceiling was not my ceiling and the super comfortable king-size bed was not my bed. My hands flew down my body. Maternity shirt? No. Bra? No. Jeans? No. Knickers? Yes! There were knickers.

My hands went up to my throbbing head, trying to think. I had flashes of me, laughing, drinking, and kissing Robin. I saw me taking off Robin's glasses and his shirt. I saw blonde Avery taking off her shirt. What?! I turned my head and looked slowly to my right. Robin's brown-haired head was laying next to me. He breathed lightly as he slept. His naked chest rose and fell. I frowned. Sitting up ever so gingerly, I peered over him. Blonde hair snuggled into Robin, on the other side. I lay back down. Chris Isaak's voice came to me, not for the first time. 'Baby Did A Bad, Bad Thing.'

I cringed. I didn't, did I?

"Please tell me you didn't," said Number One.

"You little minx!" laughed Number Two.

My brain flashed back to Moira dropping Casey and me off at the pub the previous evening. I scratched my arm as I recalled their last words.

'Go kiss a fella!' Moria had said.

And Elisa had said, 'Or a woman!'

Sinking as far down in the bed as I could, I bit my bottom lip, trying to think. Something started bubbling deep inside me, like lava, or rather, thick Toffee Apple syrup. Fat plops of Toffee Apple syrup bubbled inside. I started giggling. The syrup bubbled with more intensity and the bubbles stretched bigger and thinner until they split-splat open with a messy, "Plop!"

Lying near-naked in a strange couple's bed, my giggles turned into light laughter.

"I don't know why you're laughing," said Number One.

"Oh, lighten up!" said Number Two.

Number One sighed. "Just when you were maturing, making progress. Now, you've gone and done this! Haven't you learnt anything?"

"Yes, she's learnt how to let go and have fun, be with guys, and go with the flow," said Number Two.

"No, she hasn't learnt the fundamentals!" said Number One.

"You're fired," said Number Two.

"What?"

"You're fired," repeated Number Two. "You're too negative."

"You can't fire me, Idiot," said Number One. "I'm not going anywhere. Have you seen the situation she's gotten herself into here? She can't handle being with a woman, so what does she do? She goes for a man and a woman!"

Number Two giggled.

"How is she going to get her head around this?" said Number One.

Robin gently stroked my face. 'What's so funny?' he whispered.

'Nothing,' I whispered, looking up to the ceiling, not daring to move.

'Good morning,' he said softly.

'Hello,' I whispered.

'My name's Robin.'

'I know.'

'I know you know. I feel like we should do this right.'

'What do you mean?'

'Would you like to go out on a date with me?'

Number Two nearly burst right out of my head. "Did he just say a date?!"

Number One was not playing. "Say no. Say no. Say no!"

'Sure.'

Robin smiled, taking my hand in his.

Number One rolled her eyes. "No, no, no! Just when we thought we were getting things sorted. Seriously? You want to take another roller-coaster? Oh my Lord, you've learnt nothing; zero, zilcho, nada! You are addicted to drama!" Number One searched for ways to backtrack. "You need to slow down, wait and think. Just wait, ..."

Number Two cut in. "No wait, no nothing."

Number One had an idea. "I know! I know! What about

Doctor Soul Eyes? Let go and find him! Let's do that! Let's track him down!"

Number Two said, "Let's do right here, right now."

"Soul Eyes."

"Right here, right now."

"Soul Eyes."

"Right here, right now."

"Soul Eyes."

"Right here, right now."

I let the personality twins fight it out. I closed my eyes and snuggled into the king-size bed that wasn't mine whilst holding the hand of a very fun guy, also not mine. Bonnie Tyler's voice accompanied me as I drifted off into my dream world. I need a hero! (Certainly not a heroine.)

THE END

My dear reader

I hope you enjoyed reading Toffee Apple! I enjoyed writing it.

If you liked the book, and care to share your thoughts, would you please leave a review?I appreciate it. It helps with my author journey. (Reviews are a 'big thing' for authors. The elusive reviews! Aaaagh!)

Best wishes and continued happy reading!

Marie
Paris Connolly

More Paris Connolly books:
40 Frenchie Flirts
40 Frenchie Foodie Moments
40 Frenchie Homes

Also, there' this!
Marie Connolly Comedy on Facebook

Printed in Great Britain
by Amazon

66389148R00163